PLANNING AND DESIGNING THE DATA BASE ENVIRONMENT

PLANNING
AND DESIGNING
THE DATA BASE
ENVIRONMENT

Thomas A. Turk

VNR VAN NOSTRAND REINHOLD COMPANY
New York

Library of Congress Catalog Card Number: 84-29194
ISBN: 0-442-28528-0

Printed in the United States of America

Van Nostrand Reinhold Company Inc.
115 Fifth Avenue
New York, New York 10003

Van Nostrand Reinhold Company Limited
Molly Millars Lane
Wokingham, Berkshire RG11 2PY, England

Van Nostrand Reinhold
480 La Trobe Street
Melbourne, Victoria 3000, Australia

Macmillan of Canada
Division of Canada Publishing Corporation
164 Commander Boulevard
Agincourt, Ontario M1S 3C7, Canada

16 15 14 13 12 11 10 9 8 7 6 5 4 3 2

Library of Congress Cataloging in Publication Data

Turk, Thomas A.
  Planning and designing the data base environment.
  Bibliography: p.
  Includes index.
  1. Data base management. 2. System design. I. Title.
QA76.9.D3T86 1985   001.64   84-29194
ISBN 0-442-28528-0

This book is dedicated to all those people who have been trying to convince users and MIS personnel that data normalization is practical, efficient, and the consistent approach to designing data bases.

Special thanks goes to Bernie and Russ for their assistance in developing the physical data base designs. The person who has given me moral and technical support is my wife, Wendy. Without her this book would not have been written.

PREFACE

Data Administration is a structured approach to managing a company's information resources which insures that the company's decision makers have access to needed information, when needed. It is achieved by planning the company's data and establishing the overall logic for the company's data infrastructure. This requires the efforts of both Data Processing and end-users to identify, define, and implement the data bases which contain the company's whole data resource.

The company of the future will have its business information residing in many distributed processors. They will be connected through networks to workstations in multiple locations by an integrated set of Fourth Generation Software. The evolution to distributed processors and Fourth Generation Software requires careful strategic and tactical planning to ensure the effective and efficient use of the company's data resource. Management must commit to planning for the design and implementation of common data bases to be used by MIS-built systems, end-user-built systems and personal computers.

Historically, information systems have been designed to process and perform a specific set of functions usually devised in isolation and often collecting redundant data. The organization and other possible uses of data are often ignored or given only cursory attention; and data bases and files are built to support only those user requirements highlighted in the system's specifications. Because of this design approach, end-users are often frustrated; they are spending a lot of money on computing, they are unable to easily and readily obtain the data they need. The reason for this contradiction has not been computer hardware, but the way in which MIS projects and systems have been designed and implemented.

By continuing to build individual systems to solve individual problems, we will face these same frustrations. These problems surface in inconsistency of data stored in different systems and in limited access to data. Both flaws are related to the design of the system's data bases, files and the computer software available to the end-users for accessing the data.

Today we often find many systems providing support for a company's customer related functions. Each system has its own files or data bases containing customer data. When an end-user wants access to some specific data, MIS must first determine which file(s) or data base(s) within which system(s) contains the data since more than one file or data base may be required. MIS develops a data extract program to create a new file for the end-user to access via user-friendly software. Each new file requires maintenance and updating by MIS. In the future, the customer systems should be modified to share common data bases accessible by user-friendly software. User-friendly software and common data bases designed by the Data Planning approach will reduce MIS's need to create extract files.

The development of systems and common data bases for this environment must be done carefully. In a Fortune 500 company, a multimillion dollar Customer Information System was designed using traditional system development techniques. The project consisted of six phases of development during a three year time span. After one and a half years, the project was cancelled because the conversion system, required to migrate from the existing environment to the new environment, increased the overall cost more than a million dollars—which could have been avoided. The problem was one of incorrect phasing of the system's development. The phases were sequenced based on the needs of the end-users. However, the data required by the system was not collected until the last three phases, the belief being that a bridge system between the new system and the existing old systems could be built to supply data to the new system. This bridge is what caused the cost overrun.

During the first year of the system, the Data Models described in Chapters 3, 4 and 5 had been developed for all six phases of the system using the Data Planning approach described in Chapter 2. After the system had been canceled, the sequencing of the six phases was reviewed and found to be in error. The problem was that the data required by phase 1 was not collected until phases 4 and 6. This problem with the sequencing of the system's data requirements had been identified during Data Planning. The Entity Dependency Chart (see Chapter 2) created following normalization of the data indicated the problem would happen. It showed the need to re-sequence the system's phases. However, management had chosen to disregard the findings.

When the Customer Information System was started again with the six phases re-sequenced based on the Entity Dependencies, the original data base design was used. A significant cost and time savings occurred when the original data base design was able to support the revised system design.

To satisfy increasing requirements for data, data bases must be developed to satisfy information requirements as well as system requirements. Data base design needs to accommodate data requirements as perceived by end-users, as opposed to limited use by any particular system. The methods and procedures to build these increasingly flexible data bases are described in this book. These procedures work, but they require user-friendly software to provide access to the data. This new software is becoming available from vendors such as Cullinet, IBM, Software AG, Computer Corporation Of America and Mathematica.

Overall, Data Administration is responsible for identifying, defining, implementing and maintaining the company's long-range data plans, data resource, data inventory, data dictionary, and data bases which support end-user as well as MIS-developed system needs.

The process of implementing Data Planning is, by nature, a long-term endeavor. It requires a cultural change in the way the company builds computer-based systems, which in turn requires advanced planning, sound management and administrative control, and user-friendly software. Implementing Data Planning and Data Modeling will develop the company's data infrastructure. If started now, within five to seven years the infrastructure data bases will have been designed and many will have been implemented. This infrastructure requires an automated dictionary containing the company's inventory of data, data models, logical data structures, data security requirements, and identification of which systems collect, maintain and use the data.

Within the future data environment, it is difficult to separate Data Administration from Fourth Generation technologies. What we have are two contrasting views on the use of computers in a company. The first view is similar to our present data environment in which systems are either purchased from software vendors or created by the MIS organization using COBOL or PL/I. These systems are built based on detailed systems analysis and requirements specification developed as part of a standard Systems Development Life Cycle. In this type of company, there is usually a large application backlog. End-users try to bypass the normal system development process by obtaining their own personal computers, but are meeting with limited success.

Contrast this view with one in which Data Planning has been done: data models have been established throughout the company; data are available via data base management systems; access to data is provided via user-friendly software tools; and end-users have workstations from which they can access their data. End-users obtain data by using simple query languages designed to be as direct and English-like as possible, or by using more complex languages to make extracts from data bases and files so they can manipulate the data and ask "what-if?" questions.

Before this can happen, the data must exist and be accessible with data integrity and security ensured. A company can achieve all the foregoing ends through Data Planning, Data Modeling and Data Administration.

Thomas A. Turk

CONTENTS

PLANNING AND DESIGNING THE DATA BASE ENVIRONMENT

1. INTRODUCTION TO DATA/
DATA BASE ADMINISTRATION

INTRODUCTION

The primary problem for data processing (DP) is not a shortage of programmers, but a desire by users to get at the volumes of data in the computer. DP's inability to provide that data in a usable form to the user who needs it is the primary challenge to the industry. The problem with management information systems in the past has been that they are overwhelming. Reams of reports are produced and a manager must try to determine for himself what are the most critical pieces of information. He must do this so the necessary action can be determined to correct any problems which have occurred.

A change in Data Processing began in the late 1970s. The age of processing began to give way to the age of information. The need is not for more reports or raw data, but increased availability of information that can be accessed, understood, and used more effectively by managers.

Data/data base administration (DDBA) is established to resolve these problems. This function applies management techniques to control the company's data resource, redirects the company's system design philosophy to ensure that data serves all users, and provides the ability for end-users to directly access data they are authorized to view.

There has been tremendous growth in our capacity to collect, store, manipulate and organize data. When asked how effectively this growth has been managed, we see a data environment that is rapidly expanding, as evidenced by:

1. Redundant collection of the source data required to run the company

2. Reprocessing the same information to satisfy varying requirements
3. Proliferation of data bases and files with redundant information

Data availability and accessibility has become significant because of the growing complexity of our businesses. We need to ensure that data are available to all in the company authorized to use it. Most approaches to data base design are directed at designing for a system which processes a specific set of functions or operations. In this environment, systems are designed in isolation resulting in redundant data collection; effective organization and future uses of data have been given little consideration; data design considers only the operations on the data; and user-friendly software requests for data are difficult to handle.

Today's users expect to obtain data easily because the data have been collected, but this is not always possible. Satisfying growing information needs requires the development of more flexible data bases which reflect the relations between the data as perceived by the end-users, not by a system.

DATA PLANNING

The data base environment of today consists of micro computers networked to mini and mainframe computers (Fig. 1-1). In this configuration, data are collected from source locations and distributed to the locations where they are needed. Making data available while providing data integrity, security, and minimized redundancy requires a plan which describes the data architecture required for this environment. Much effort has been and will be expended to build networks for this distributed processing environment. Private line versus dial-up, LANs, controllers, protocols, and vendors are of primary concern. What are we trying to get from one location to another? Data. Do we plan for this? Seldom!

Before designing networks, selecting computer hardware or building systems, a data plan is necessary which identifies and defines:

1. The major business functions of the company
2. The data required to support these business functions
3. How data are to be structured for the company, not for a specific system

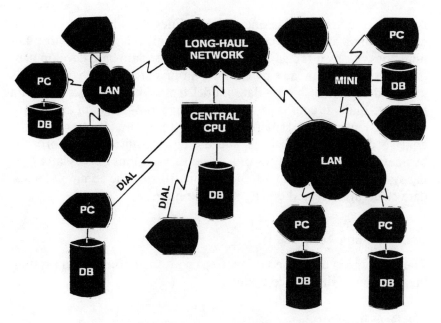

Fig. 1-1. Today's data base environment.

4. The sequence in which data are created
5. The sources of data

With this information, better decisions can be made when selecting a network architecture and computer hardware and building computer systems. If the designer knows what is needed, where it is needed, and how frequently, a better network will be designed. Knowing the data required by a location plus the system's requirements permits better hardware selection. History has shown that network, hardware, and systems change frequently. However, the company's data architecture seldom changes. When it does, it is the result of a change in the company, e.g., an acquisition, divestiture, or fundamental change in how business is conducted.

Data Planning Guidelines

Data planning provides a synergistic approach using data normalization techniques to create data structures which satisfy end-user needs, reduce system development expense, and minimize data redundancy.

A synergistic approach is one which defines the whole environment and then breaks it into its components for implementation. Data planning does this by establishing the direction for data base development throughout the company by creating an inventory of the company's data and by establishing a data model from which all files and data bases are built. It emphasizes the need for front-end data analysis to establish logical data structures for the company. It integrates the analysis of business functions and the data required to perform the business functions. Analysis of a system's functions occurs later during system development with the system utilizing the common logical data structures created during data planning.

Data Planning Activities

The planning is composed of six steps with their completion producing and identifying the company's:

- Data inventory
- Normalized data model
- Data dependencies
- Common logical data structures (structural data model)
- Source systems for data

The six steps for establishing data planning are to:

1. Determine the business functions and the business model which identifies manual and mechanized systems which support the functions
2. Identify the data items required by each business function and develop the business function's normalized data model
3. Determine the dependencies that exist among the normalized entities and chart the dependency flow required for creating and updating entities
4. Determine the logical data structures
5. Identify basic volume information for the normalized data
6. Determine the business function which is the source for each normalized entity and which system should be the source system

DATA MODEL DEVELOPMENT

Data base design can be done more quickly and effectively using data modeling techniques. These techniques translate a theoretical model, called the *normalized data model,* to a physical data base which can be implemented in any of the current data base management systems (DBMSs). A total of three data models (normalized, usage, and structural) are developed during data planning or early in the development of a system. In either case the models and the physical data base design are completed before the programs are designed. The resulting physical data base design can be for micro, mini or mainframe computers. The decision does not need to be made until the structural data model is developed.

Normalized Data Model

The normalized data model identifies relations between data elements and organizes them into logical groupings called *entities.* The process requires data to be normalized based on the user environment, not the system. Normalization is defined as:

> The process of breaking down complex end-user views of data into simple data structures that can be represented in two-dimensional arrays or tables.

Normalizing the data structures satisfies the company's information requirements and reduces the possibility of change to the structures when information requirements change. Since data relations are based on the user environment, the normalized data model is common to all systems using the same data or a subset of the data. It is better to normalize data for a business function rather than for a system because this represents more end-users' views of the data. A system's view is limited to the specific business needs being satisfied. Normalization involves:

1. Identifying primary keys
2. Identifying repeating data items
3. Identifying data items in an entity which are not functionally dependent on all data items composing its primary key

4. Identifying data items uniquely identified by the entity's primary key which are actually dependent on another data item in the entity (transitive dependency)

Two products document the normalized data model. The first is the *entity–data item list* which documents the content of each normalized entity. The second product is a pictorial representation of the entities and relations between the entities. This *linkage diagram* is used as a walkthrough tool for reviewing the data with the user and in developing the structural data model.

Usage Data Model

The usage data model collects high-level business usage information to performance tune physical data base design. It identifies what data are accessed and how often they are accessed based on the perspective of the end-user's, not of the data processing personnel. This ensures that the physical data base reflects end-user needs, not just processing efficiency. The steps to develop the model are to:

1. Identify volume estimates
2. Determine logical access requirements
3. Related usage to the normalized data model

Volume estimates define the number of occurrences of each entity and relation. The logical access requirements are identified during system analysis to identify which normalized entities and relations are required by the system. Relating usage to the normalized data model ensures that all data required by the system are contained in the model.

The usage data model is used to select the subset of the normalized data model required by a system or set of systems. It is input for physical data base design decisions. If a limited view of usages is presented, a data base serving those limited usages is created. Adding additional access requirements at a later time may cause changes to the physical data base design. In order to develop a flexible data base, one should look at current and future uses of the data when developing this model. This is critical when a system is developed in phases or the data are planned to be used by other systems. The resulting data base design will be flexible enough to meet unknown usages with minimal change.

Structural Data Model

The structural data model is created from the normalized data model by manipulating the normalized data model's linkage diagram to produce logical data structures. Seven steps translate the normalized data into logical data structures that can be implemented by a nonrelational data base management system (DBMS):

1. Resolve implied relations
2. Modify many-to-many relations
3. Modify identity relations
4. Identify potentially redundant entities
5. Identify roots
6. Identify the pseudo-roots
7. Develop the logical structures

For a relational data base management system three steps are followed to produce the table definitions:

1. Resolve identity relations
2. Resolve one-to-many relations
3. Resolve many-to-many relations

Physical Data Base Design

Physical data base design requires the normalized data model, usage data model, structural data model, and knowledge of the chosen DMBS. The data base administrator (physical data base designer) uses the modeling tools of the DBMS and the data models to design the physical data base. If no DBMS modeling tools exist, you must rely upon the knowledge of the data base administrator. In physical design the normalized entities become segments or repeating groups and relations become the hierarchical or network mappings. The structural data model depicts the ideal physical implementation. However, redundancy needs to be resolved and performance considerations applied. This book does not define the modeling efforts required to develop the physical design. This information is available from the various DBMS vendors. What is important is that:

1. The segments, repeating groups, or tables have been defined
2. The relations (mappings) have been defined
3. Usage information is available for modeling

A data base administrator knowledgeable in the DBMS is a must. The data models help in shortening design time and provide for a physical data base completed prior to program design. These techniques have been used to design data bases quickly and efficiently many DBMSs.

DATA/DATA BASE ADMINISTRATION

Data/data base administration (DDBA) is the function responsible for centralizing the management of the company's data resource. It involves many specialized skills such as planning, system analysis, data modeling, data base design, security controls, physical storage organization, recovery implementation, and auditing. These skills are performed by one person or many people depending on the size of the management information system (MIS) organization and the complexity of the data bases being built.

Management of the data resource is centralized in order to provide a well planned and controlled implementation of the company's data base environment. To achieve this, the DDBA function is divided between two groups: data administration and data base administration. Their responsibilities range from custody of the data resource to control over its content, use, and availability.

Data Administration

Data administration (DA) is responsible for identifying and defining the company's inventory of data, establishing the company's data plan, and developing and documenting the company's and system's normalized, usage, and structural data models. The non–data base management system (non-DBMS) technical activities required to manage the company's data resource are the responsibility of the data administration group.

Data Base Administration

Decisions and activities on the technical design and implementation of data bases are the responsibility of the data base administration (DBA) group. These decisions and activities include:

1. Design of the DBMS logical and physical data base structures
2. Establishing data base access methods and strategies
3. Monitoring and optimizing data base performance
4. Establishing data base access authorization and security procedures
5. Documenting technical data base design information in the data dictionary
6. Technical DBMS support to end-user system development and maintenance personnel

Organization

Placement of data/data base administration (DDBA) within the company should be at a level where it has equal authority with the systems development and computer operations organizations (see Fig. 1-2). This placement includes the authority to direct and control data base development within all organizations and systems. It centralizes activities related to data planning, data modeling, and data base design, implementation, operation, and control. Even when system development is decentralized the DDBA function should be centralized. Data bases are decentralized or centralized to fit with the needs of the business. Data constitute a company resource which should be managed like any other company resource.

Distributed data processing environments need centralized DDBA organization because data planning, data inventory, and data modeling provides common logical data structures for all locations requiring the same or a subset of the same data. Local systems are tailored to local needs and use the subset of the common logical data structures

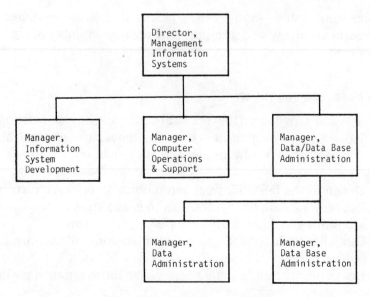

Fig. 1-2. Organization structure.

which supports local data requirements. Implementing common logical data structures in local systems enables a centralized computer or a user to easily poll the various local data bases and gather the required data.

Implementation

To implement data/data base administration, the following activities are performed:

1. Implement a company data policy by obtaining company-wide commitment to data/data base administration (DDBA). This includes establishing the DDBA organization and its charter and the development of required tasks and responsibilities.
2. Create a data inventory using standard terminology for the company and document it in a centralized data dictionary/directory. This dictionary/directory contains standardized data item names and definitions as well as source system(s) for each data item, and identifies using systems.

3. Develop the company's normalized data models for each of its business functions based on the end-users' perspective of the data.
4. As new systems are identified, extract the system's normalized data model from the company's and develop the system's usage and structural data models.

Benefits of DDBA

Implementing these activities results in positioning the company to actively compete beyond the 1980s. This competitive position is achieved by:

1. Providing management with the data they need when they need it to make better business decisions
2. Reducing the cost of collecting, maintaining and providing data by sharing data between systems and users
3. Increasing data security and auditing capabilities

Better Decision Making. Today there is seldom a single source for identifying all data maintained in the company, which systems collect, update, or use it, or the data names and definitions. A data inventory is established to provide a centralized repository of data about data; this enables a user or MIS person to find out where a data item exists, its definition and allowable values, and its security requirements. This inventory provides more consistent information to systems development or end-users when building systems used to make business decisions.

Implementing data planning includes creating the company's data inventory, building data models, and establishing common logical data structures. This leads to a data processing environment which provides consistent information to all who require the data, and the hardware environment needed to satisfy the requirements of the business.

Reducing Costs. Data planning, which includes building a data inventory and establishing data models and common logical data structures for business functions, is about 75 percent of the data base design effort. This is done once for the company, not once for each system in the company. The remaining 25 percent is physical data base design, which is done for each system which has its own data base. The savings in development time and personnel time is tremendous.

If two systems are built using data bases which contain 50 percent of the same data items and the data base design time for each system is 100 person days, 50 person days of redundant effort occurred. This time could be better used in satisfying other business requirements.

Sharing Data. Logical data structures based upon the company's view of data results in identification of data that can be shared. Developing data bases based on these structures enables a system developer and data administrator to evaluate the ability of the system to use existing data bases. The data inventory documented in the data dictionary/directory provides the necessary information to make the decisions.

Increasing Data Security and Auditability. A dictionary/directory will document security requirements and whose authorization is required before an individual or system can access data. Access authorization to the data base is tightly controlled by the data / data base administration (DDBA) group. They provide systems and end-users with access to only the data they are authorized to view or update. In addition, DBA monitors data access and reports to management attempts by systems and end-users to access data they are not authorized to access.

CONCLUSION

Data underly the information explosion. Providing data requires its collection, maintenance, and structuring so that all who need it and are authorized to have it can get it when they need it. This requires a well planned, well managed, and integrated data processing environment. Actually, integration is not the correct term. Integration merely implies that you combine pieces to make the whole. The environment should be synergistic—i.e., the whole is greater than the sum of its parts.

Data planning creates the whole first, then system development breaks it into pieces for implementation. Data planning defines the business functions and detailed data required to support them. System planning efforts use the data planning results to determine the network, hardware, and information systems required to support the business's information requirements. Business functions and data are the foundation because they are stable. This synergistic approach allows the impact of new technology to be evaluated as to its effect on the business and information requirements. The areas which can benefit from new technology are identified and then presented to the end-users and system development personnel, in the areas affected, for their consideration and action.

2. DATA PLANNING

INTRODUCTION

Data planning is a synergistic approach to identifying and defining the company's data environment. It uses data analysis techniques to separate the logical design of data bases from the System Development process and from physical data base design. Data Planning establishes a detailed inventory of the company's data as viewed by end-users and establishes logical data structures for system development. These logical data structures are usable by multiple systems and can be implemented in any micro-, mainframe, or minicomputer DBMS.

Data planning requires the analysis of business functions, analysis of the data required to perform the business functions and the development of three data models: normalized, usage, and structural. Following completion of data planning, systems analysis is performed to identify systems which satisfy the end-users processing requirements. Data planning forms a foundation for system development by establishing the logical data structures those systems will use. System functions and processes are important, but should be built to utilize the logical data structures. Over time these data structures are more stable because they are based on the business (end-user) requirements, not on a system's requirements. These structures remain unchanged when system processing changes. Logical data structures do change when the company changes the way it does business.

Data Planning consists of six steps:

1. Determine business functions and the business model which identifies manual and mechanized systems which support the functions.
2. Identify what data items are required by each business function and develop the business function's normalized data model.

3. Determine dependencies that exist among the normalized entities and chart the dependency flow required for creating and updating entities.
4. Determine the logical data structures.
5. Identify basic volume information for the normalized data.
6. Determine the business function which is the source for each normalized entity and which system should be the source system.

Steps 2–6 are performed for each business function with analysis in one step identifying the need for additional analysis in preceding steps.

Unlike most system, business, or data planning approaches, such as IBM's Business System Planning (BSP), this data planning approach collects detailed data items and stresses *data* not systems, problem analysis, or the development of a high-level view of the entire company. This data planning approach results in a general business model of each major functional area of the business with enough detail to ensure that a detailed data model can be developed. The data model is a logical design of the data that can be implemented in any data base management system currently available.

DATA PLANNING APPROACH

Determine Business Functions and Business Model

The first step identifies the business functions and its business processes for the company and the current or planned systems which support these functions. A business function is a high-level activity which is descriptive of the basic activities or processes performed in the company. Normally a business function is the responsibility of a single organization within the company; however, it can be shared between organizations. Some examples are: finance, marketing, purchasing, and inventory control. A set of basic Business Functions for a manufacturing business is shown in Fig. 2-1. Within each of these business functions, business processes are identified and defined.

Using the business functions and processes, prepare a matrix with business processes within business function across the top, and proposed and current systems down the left side. This matrix is used to identify which systems support each business process and which busi-

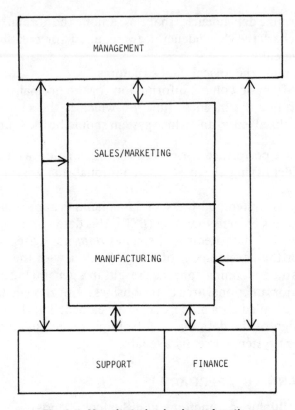

Fig. 2-1. Manufacturing business functions.

ness processes are supported by more than one system. In addition it is used to highlight the systems being developed or modified within the next 12–24 months. As each business process or system is identified, a brief narrative description is written. Agreement on these descriptions must be reached prior to continuing the planning process. All people involved must have the same definition for each system and business function. An example of the business process/system matrix is shown in Fig. 2-2.

Identify Data Inventory and Develop the Normalized Data Model

The second step identifies the data required to support each business function and establishes the company's inventory of data and the underlying structure of the data called the normalized data model.

Businss Functions	System 1	System 2	System 3	System n

Fig. 2-2. Business function/system matrix.

Creating the data inventory requires interviews with end-users to determine additional current and future data requirements to support each business function. All current manual and mechanized system source documents are reviewed to verify and complete the data inventory. When reviewing existing systems which partially or wholly perform the business function, caution should be exercised because these sources will identify derivable data items. Derivable data can cause unnecessary confusion and complexity because much of it will change as user needs change. What needs to be identified are the data items used to create the derivable data. A derivable data item is included in data modeling when the items used to derive it are not contained in the business function's data inventory. Whether or not derived data are included in the data base is based on the data access and processing requirements defined during system development.

As data items are identified, each is documented in the data dictionary/directory with a unique name and clear definition. In addition, the business function(s) which create or update it and the systems which contain it are documented. Fig. 2–3 shows a sample data dictionary/directory entry for a data item. The data in the data inventory are analyzed for synonyms and homonyms, as well as mutually exclusive and derivable data, all of which are removed or resolved. This ensures that each data item is unique, and compound data items are broken into their component data items. Details on the process are described in Chapter 3, in the section on creating the data inventory.

Individual data items are logically related to each other based on how the business uses the data. These relationships are identified by a process called *normalization*. In normalization, data are grouped together and assigned a unique label according to a predefined set of rules. This process, defined in Chapter 3, produces groupings of data, called *entities,* and the relations (relationships) between the entities. Creating this normalized data model defines the ideal structure for a data base. It is documented by detailed lists of entities and its data item contents, defining the relations between entities, and a pictorial representation of the entities and relations called the linkage diagram (see Fig. 2–4).

Data Item Name:	Customer Number
Description:	A descriptive code identifying a Customer and its subsidiaries. The first 3 characters identify the parent company and the last 4 identify the subsidiary. If there are no subsidiaries the last 4 characters are '000A'.
Derivation:	Not Applicable
Standard Value Set:	7 characters
Format:	AAN–NNNA
Composed Of:	Parent Company Number Subsidiary Number

Fig. 2–3. Data dictionary/directory entry.

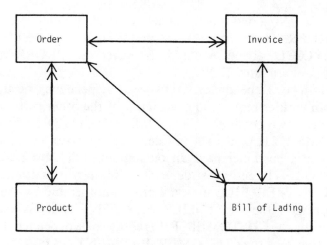

Fig. 2-4. Linkage diagram.

In Fig. 2-4 the lines with the arrowheads are relations and the rectangles represent entities. A relation shows that one entity is related to another entity as defined by the end-user. The arrowheads indicate whether the related entity will have one or more than one sets of data values given one set of values for the other entity. Fig. 2-4 indicates that each ORDER entity can have many INVOICE entity occurrences (double arrowhead) for one occurrence of the ORDER entity. For each occurrence of the INVOICE entity, only zero or one ORDER entity occurrence (single arrowhead) can exist.

Determine Entity Dependencies

Once entities and relations between the entities are identified, the dependencies between them are identified (step 3). A dependency identifies that an occurrence of one entity must exist before an occurrence of the other entity can exist. For every relation between two entities, a dependency also exists between them and the direction of the dependency is identified. There are two types of dependencies:

1. One-Way Dependency. A one-way dependency occurs when one entity requires an occurrence of the other entity to exist before an occurrence of the original entity can exist. In the linkage diagram

in Fig. 2–4, a one-way dependency exist between INVOICE and ORDER. This is true because an ORDER must exist before an INVOICE can be prepared. However, an ORDER can exist without a related INVOICE.

2. Two-Way Dependency. A two-way dependency occurs when both entities require an occurrence of the other entity to exist. Given two entities, CUSTOMER PAYMENT and CUS-TOMER BILL, a two-way dependency exists between them. When a customer pays an outstanding bill the CUSTOMER PAYMENT entity is dependent upon the existence of a CUSTOMER BILL entity. Before another bill is issued to a customer, the CUSTOMER PAYMENT entity is examined, causing the CUSTOMER BILL entity to be dependent upon the existence of the CUSTOMER PAYMENT entity.

Each relation in the normalized data model is evaluated by deter-mining the relation's primary entity, and the direction of the depen-dency. For each relation ask one of the following questions:

- Is one entity required by the business function to create or deter-mine the other entity?
- Which entity is logically necessary first?

This establishes which of the two entities is the primary entity and which is the dependent entity. If neither entity satisfies questions, then a two-way dependency exists. Once the primary entity is determined, ask:

Does the passage of time within the business function appear to reverse the direction of the dependency?

If yes, there is a two-way dependency between the entities. If no, there is a one-way dependency from the primary entity to the other entity. The dependencies shown in Fig. 2–5 were based on the end-users an-swering the data dependency questions for the linkage diagram of Fig. 2–4.

The linkage diagram is modified by drawing a circle around the ar-rowhead(s) pointing into the dependent entity, as shown in Fig. 2–6. If

RELATIONSHIP	DEPENDENCY ENTITY	PRIMARY
Order to Invoice	One-way	Order
Order and Product	One-way	Product
Order and Bill-of-Lading	One-way	Order
Invoice and Bill-of-Lading	Two-way	Invoice and Bill-of-Lading

Fig. 2–5. Entity data dependency table.

it is a two-way dependency, draw circles around the arrowheads at both ends of the relation. Fig. 2–7 shows an alternative to using the linkage diagram. This PERT chart format works effectively for large normalized data models.

Determine Logical Data Structures

Creating logical data structures (step 4) translates the normalized data model into structures which can be implemented in hierarchical, network, or relational data base management systems. Chapter 5 defines in detail the process for creating logical data structures.

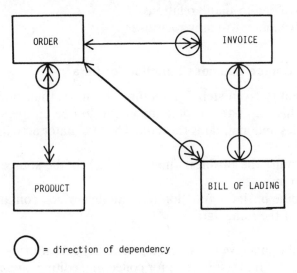

Fig. 2–6. Linkage diagram data dependency diagram.

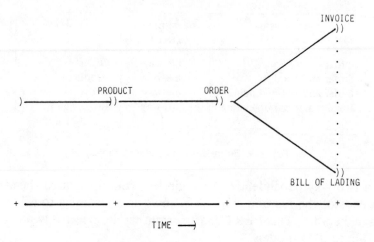

Fig. 2-7. PERT data dependency diagram.

For hierarchical or network DBMS, seven steps are required to develop the structural data model while relational DBMSs require only three steps:

1. Resolve identity relations
2. Resolve one-to-many relations
3. Resolve many-to-many relations

Determine Source Business Function for Data

When an entity from step 2 is required by more than one business function, this step (step 5) determines the source business function which creates and maintains the data. The two major activities are to:

1. Determine the business function which is the source for each data item
2. Combine business function data models which contain at least 75% of the same data

Custodial rights give a system responsibility for ensuring the integrity of the data. It is responsible for collecting, editing, and maintaining the data. It gives the system responsibility to supply data to other systems either by providing access to its data base or by providing a file containing the data.

Common logical data structures are identified by using the system–business-function matrix from step 1. When a business function is supported by two or more systems, the systems should share data. If those systems support another business function, include its data in the common logical data structures. These systems can be within one organization or similar systems in different organizations. When a common logical data structure is identified, it can consist of one or more data models. If only one data model is identified, it is used to create the common logical data structure. When more than one data model is identified, they are merged into a common data model which is used to create the common logical data structure(s).

Reevaluate source documents from step 2 to determine which business function creates and maintains each data item. Each item has one source business function and one or more which may use it. For the entities in the example of step 2, the source business functions are:

Order Entry	for Order
Invoices	for Invoice
Design and Development	for Product
Picking	for Bill of Lading

This information is added to the data dictionary/directory documentation.

Review and analyze the business function's normalized data model to identify if the models contain duplicate data. When two or more data models contain at least 75% of the same data, combine them. This decreases the number of models needed to support the business and results in reducing the number of potential data bases, and minimizing data redundancy.

INTEGRATING WITH SYSTEMS PLANNING

Review the long-range system plans to determine the sequence in which systems are planned to be built. Determine the logical data structures required by each system using the entity dependency diagram (step 3) to determine if the entities included a system have dependencies on entities not included. If there are some, the system's scope should be expanded to either collect and maintain the data in those entities or to obtain the data from another system that is implemented or will be implemented first. When the entities do not exist in another system, that system becomes the source for those data. As a source system it becomes responsible for collecting, editing, and maintaining the data and supplying it to other systems which need the data. A review of systems which greatly exceeded cost and time estimates found that many of them failed initially to expand their scope to include the primary entities. The cost and time overrun was due to the necessity to include these entities and the additional programs required after the system development was underway.

The long-range system plan should be adjusted to reflect the data dependencies either by expanding the scope of the systems or by resequencing the systems to be developed so the source systems are built first. Resequencing is preferable to expanding the system's scope, but it incurs political problems.

During the development of a source system, the business function's normalized data model, usage information (defined in Chapter 4), and logical data structures are used to build its data base. When another system is developed that requires data from the source system and other data not included in the system, the normalized data models are reviewed and common logical data structures are identified. The source system's data base is expanded to include the new entities and the physical data base is modified to service both systems or a second data base is created for the new system. If a second data base is built, the common logical data structure(s) are used. Creating, editing, and maintaining data which are redundantly stored in the second data base is the responsibility of the source system either by directly updating the second system's data base or by providing a periodic dump and load. Performance requirements of each system must be evaluated to determine which is used.

3. NORMALIZED DATA MODEL

INTRODUCTION

This chapter presents a method for developing a normalized data model to describe the company's data environment. The Normalized Data Model structures data for the company by identifying relationships between data. Since the relationships between data are based on the user environment, the normalized data structure is common to all systems using the same data or a subset of the data. Defining these enables one to produce a controlled, up-to-date, accurate model of the company's data and a physical data base which has minimal data redundancy and increased data integrity.

Development of the model begins and ends prior to systems analysis. Changes can occur as a result of system analysis, but these changes usually have a minor impact on the normalized data model.

Normalization creates entity–data item lists in which all data items are dependent on the primary key of the entities. The primary key is defined as one or more data items which are required to uniquely identify an entity. For example, Social Security Number is the primary key for an entity called PERSON. If a data item in an entity has more than one occurrence for a single occurrence of the primary key, this repeating data item is removed from the entity and placed in a new entity. During normalization data items are added to or removed from entities according to the rules of normalization. After normalization is complete, data items should not have to be moved from one entity to another. Because of this, the time and manpower required to maintain the physical data bases and the programs accessing the data bases is significantly reduced when data bases are designed from the normalized data model.

Normalization involves four steps:

1. Identifying primary keys
2. Identifying repeating data items
3. Identifying data items in an entity which are not functionally dependent on all data items which compose its primary key
4. Identifying data items that are uniquely identified by the entity's primary key and another data item in the entity

CREATING THE DATA INVENTORY

During data planning or systems analysis identify and define the data required to establish a data inventory for the company or system. Development begins by examining:

1. Long-range system plans
2. Documentation of existing mechanized data bases/files
3. Existing and proposed source and report information
4. Existing data dictionaries

The most important source is interviews with end-users and systems analysts who can provide information on what is, should be, or will exist now and in the future. There are three steps to developing the data inventory:

1. Develop an entity list
2. Develop entity–data item lists
3. Resolve the entity–data item lists

An entity is defined as a person, place, thing or event such as:

EMPLOYEE	ASSET	CUSTOMER
PRODUCT	PART	VENDOR
INVOICE	BILL	TARIFF
LOCATION	LEGISLATION	INVENTORY

Entities are inherent to the company and as such they require end-users to identify them. Begin by asking various users to list possible entities. Do not review it for redundancy or relevance since later steps in the normalization process identifies, merges, or removes inconsistencies.

After entities are identified, prepare a list of data items for each entity. As data items are identified each is documented with its name, description/definition and standard-value-set. A data item can be found in more than one entity at this stage of development. Fig. 3–1 shows an example of an entity–data item list.

As each data item for an entity is identified, it is given a meaningful name and placed in the entity–data item list. Problems do occur with data naming and definitions. One problem is that different users have different meanings for the same data name. For example, a data item called "Name" can have a variety of meanings. In a personnel system, it is the name of the employee and in an inventory system, the name of the product. Given a company's view of data, each data item must be qualified. For the personnel system, "Name" becomes "Employee Name" and for the Inventory System it becomes "Product Name." The data item Name in Fig. 3–1 is changed to Product Name.

To clarify a data item's name, each is given a brief but clear description/definition written in end-user terminology. In addition, the data item's standard value set is identified. This specifies the allowable values for a data item expressed as discrete values, ranges, or number and type of characters, as shown in Fig. 3–2.

When most of the entity–data item lists are created, begin reviewing them for homonyms, synonyms, and derived or mutually exclusive data items. Resolving and removing these completes the data inventory. Each data item's definition and standard value set should be documented in a data dictionary/directory.

Entity Name: ORDER
Description: A list of items made by our company ordered by a customer
Data Items: Order Number   Customer Name
              Name   Customer Number
              Product Description   Customer Address
              Product Number   Shipping Address
              Quantity Ordered   UPS
              Unit Price   Express
              Total Product Price   Surface
              Merchandise Total   Gross Sale Dollars
              Delivery Charge   Order Sales Tax
              Total Order Cost   Order Date

Fig. 3–1. Entity-data item list.

Entity Name: ORDER

DATA ITEM	STANDARD VALUE SET
Customer Address	60 characters
Customer Name	25 characters
Customer Number	7 characters, AAN–NNNA
Delivery Charge	$999.99
Express	1 character, letter E
Merchandise Total Cost	$999,999.99
Order Date	mm/dd/yy
Order Number	6 characters, AANNNA
Order Sales Tax	$9,999.99
Parcel Post	1 character, letter P
Product Description	25 alphanumeric characters.
Product Name	25 alphanumeric characters.
Product Number	10 alphanumeric characters.
Quantity Ordered	4 characters, signed integer
Shipping Address	60 characters
Surface	1 character, letter S
Total Order Cost	$999,999.99
Total Product Price	$99,999.99
UPS	1 character, letter U
Unit Price	$9,999.99

Fig. 3–2. Standard value set.

Homonyms

Homonyms are defined as the same name used for data with different definitions. They are fairly easy to identify since they have the same data item names and different descriptions, different standard value set, or both. They are handled by reviewing the description and standard value sets. If they are different data items, qualify their data name. If they are the same, combine them and give the new data item a meaningful name and merge their descriptions and standard value sets. Be careful when relying on standard value sets to identify homonyms because the same data item can have different lengths or representations.

If, as in Fig. 3–3, the data item names and standard value sets are the same but the descriptions are different, one or both data item names are changed. The Name which describes a product is changed

DATA ITEM NAME	DESCRIPTION	STANDARD VALUE SET
Name	Last name, first name, middle initial of a person	Alphanumeric less than 20 characters
Name	Name given to describe a product	Alphanumeric less than 20 characters

Fig. 3-3. Homonym example.

to Product Name. The other is changed to Employee Name. It is necessary to be specific and use appropriate qualifiers in naming data items to avoid current and future confusion.

Synonyms

Synonyms are defined as different data item names used to identify the same data item. Concurrence on one data item name is obtained for synonyms, with the other names documented as a synonym or alias. Identifying synonyms is done by reviewing data items for similar names, descriptions, or standard value sets and then reviewing the possible synonyms with the end-user.

In Fig. 3-4, both data items (Product Name and Product Description) have the same standard value set and a similar description. Here one should go back to the end-user to determine if they are synonyms. If they are, they should be combined under one name, with the other listed as a synonym or alias. If not, both items are retained in the data inventory and the description is clarified as shown in Fig. 3-4.

Derived Data

A data item whose value can be created from one or more other data items is defined as a derived data item. Identify the data items used to derive it, and how they are combined to create it. Derivable data items are identified and included in the development of the data models. In the entity–data item lists, each derivable data item is prefixed by 'D'. The decision to store or derive is made during physical data base design.

Initial Description

DATA ITEM NAME	DESCRIPTION	STANDARD VALUE SET
Billing Point	The company location which produces the customer's bill	4 numeric characters
Location Code	A code which identifies each office, factory, etc. in the company	4 numeric characters

Changed Description

DATA ITEM NAME	DESCRIPTION	STANDARD VALUE SET
Billing Point	An accounting department assigned code which identifies the location which produced the customer's bill	4 numeric characters
Location Code	A code assigned by the personnel department which identifies each office, factory, etc. in the company	4 numeric characters

Fig. 3–4. Synonym example.

An example of derivable data is Age, defined as current age of a person. Given data items Birth Date and Current Date, Age can be derived. How it is derived is documented with its description.

Figure 3-5 shows the modifications to the entity–data item list for derivable data, homonyms, and synonyms.

Mutually Exclusive Data

When only one of several possible data items can exist for a given occurrence of an entity, these data items are defined as mutually exclusive. Mutually exclusive data items are combined and given a name meaningful to the end-user. In Fig. 3–2, four mutually exclusive data items exist in the ORDER entity. UPS, Parcel Post, Express, and Surface, which represent the shipping mode, are mutually exclusive since only one can exist for a given ORDER. Their descriptions and standard value sets are combined to form the description and standard value set for the new data item Shipping Mode. For the purpose of normalization, the four data items are deleted from the entity–data item list and Shipping Mode is inserted (see Fig. 3–5).

Data Item and Entity Definition

DATA ITEM NAME	DEFINITION
Total Product Price	The total cost of one item purchased by a customer. DERIVABLE: Quantity Ordered times Unit Price. STANDARD VALUE SET: $99,999.99
Merchandise Total	The total cost of all items purchased by a customer, not including costs associated with the order in general. DERIVABLE: Sum of Quantity Ordered times Unit Price for all products on an order. STANDARD VALUE SET: $999,999.99
Total Order Cost	The total cost of all items purchased by a customer including costs associated with the order. DERIVABLE: Sum of Quantity Ordered times Unit Price for all products on an order, then add to it the Delivery Charge and Order Sales Tax. STANDARD VALUE SET: $999,999.99

Entity Name: ORDER

Description: A list of items made by our company ordered by a Customer

Data Items:

Order Number	Customer Name
Product Name	Customer Number
Product Description	Customer Address
Product Number	Shipping Address
Quantity Ordered	Shipping Mode
Unit Price	'D' Total Product Price
Delivery Charge	'D' Merchandise Total Cost
Order Sales Tax	'D' Total Order Cost
Order Date	

Fig. 3–5. Resolved data inventory example.

Resolving synonyms, homonyms, derived data, and mutually exclusive data provides the company with a common set of data called a data inventory. The data descriptions are usable by all systems within the company which require those data.

NORMALIZATION

The normalized data model creates a data structure for the company which identifies the relationships between data items. The structure created by normalizing data will satisfy the company's information requirements and reduce the possibility of change to the structures when information needs change. Since data relations are based on the end-user environment, the normalized data model is common to all systems using the same data or a subset of the data if data are normalized for a business function rather than a system. This allows the data administrator to utilize information collected for many systems as input to normalization.

The three levels of normalization are:

1. First Normal Form—Identifying primary keys and repeating data items
2. Second Normal Form—Identifying data items in an entity which are not functionally dependent on all data items composing its primary key
3. Third Normal Form—Identifying data items uniquely identified by the entity's primary key which are actually dependent some other data item in the entity (transitive dependency)

First Normal Form

First normal form identifies the entity's primary key and removes repeating data items. During this process new entities are created to contain the repeating data items. One or more data items can be required to uniquely identify an occurrence of an entity. There may be more than one set of data items which uniquely identify an occurrence of the entity. When this occurs, each set of data items is called a *candidate key*. A *primary key* is the candidate key selected to uniquely identify an entity for the purpose of normalization. The three steps of normalization are based on a data item's relationship to the entity's primary key.

The rules for choosing a primary key when there are two or more candidate keys are:

1. If a candidate key is composed of more than one data item, and one or more of its data items can have unknown (null) values at the same time, it cannot be the primary key.
2. Choose the candidate key most frequently used by the end-user.

make sure it is unique. For example: "Employee Name" may not be unique, but "Employee Number" or "Social Security Number" are.

3. If you cannot determine which is most frequently used, choose the one composed of the fewest data items.
4. Last, the end-user selects the primary key.

Using Fig. 3–5, only one data item is a candidate key: Order Number. Since there is only one candidate key it is also the primary key. The primary key in the entity–data item list is prefixed by 'PK' and the candidate keys are underlined. If two or more candidate keys are identified by the end-user, one must be chosen based on the rules previously defined. There are cases where more than one data item is required to uniquely identify an entity. For example, a WORK AS-SIGNMENT entity contains the following data items:

Employee Number   Project Name
Employee Name   Project Code
Assignment Description   Assignment Estimated Duration
Actual Time Worked On   Percentage Complete
   Assignment
Assignment Due Date

The user defines Employee Name, Employee Number, Project Name, and Project Code as data items which make up the candidate keys. To select the one or more data items which make the WORK ASSIGNMENT entity unique, the user defines the following candidate key combinations:

- Employee Name and Project Name
- Employee Name and Project Code
- Employee Number and Project Name
- Employee Number and Project Code

Since only one set can be the primary key, the rules selected Employee Number and Project Code. Both data items are marked with the prefix 'PK' in the entity–data item list and all four data items are underlined.

After completing the selection of primary keys, you may find entities which have the same candidate key or primary key. When this occurs, combine them before continuing normalization.

Any nonprimary key data item that can have multiple values for a given occurrence of a primary key is identified and called a *repeating data item*. Repeating data items are grouped together to form a repeating group if for a given occurrence of the primary key, any of the repeating data items occur the same number of times. Each repeating data item is prefixed by 'R' as shown in Fig. 3–6. The six repeating data items in Fig. 3–6 are grouped into one repeating group containing: Product Name, Product Description, Product Number, Quantity Ordered, Unit Price, and Total Product Price.

Once the repeating data items or repeating groups are identified, normalization requires their removal from the entity and placement in a new entity. The new entity contains the removed data items and the primary key of the entity from which they were removed. The repeating group of Fig. 3–6 is placed in a new entity called PRODUCT ORDER, with the primary key from the ORDER entity as shown in Fig. 3–7. The primary key of the new entity contains the primary key data items from the original entity. However, the new entity's primary

---

Entity Name: ORDER

Description: A list of items made by our company ordered by a customer

Data Items:

'PK' Order Number	Customer Name
'R' Product Name	Customer Number
'R' Product Description	Customer Address
'R' Product Number	Shipping Address
'R' Quantity Ordered	Shipping Mode
'R' Unit Price	'R' 'D' Total Product Price
Delivery Charge	'D' Merchandise Total Cost
Order Sales Tax	'D' Total Order Cost
Order Date	

'PK' Indicates that the data item is part of or the entire primary key.

'R' This data item can have more than one value for one value of the primary key data item(s).

'D' This indicates that the data item can be derived from one or more data items.

Fig. 3–6. Keys and repeating data identified.

Entity Name: PRODUCT ORDER

Description: Information on an order for product(s) purchased by a customer

Data Items:
'PK' Order Number	'PK' Product Number
Product Name	Product Description
Quantity Ordered	Unit Price
'D' Total Product Price	

Entity Name: ORDER

Description: A list of items made by our company ordered by a customer

Data Items:
'PK' Order Number	Customer Name
Order Sales Tax	Customer Number
Order Date	Customer Address
Shipping Address	'D' Merchandise Total Cost
Delivery Charge	Shipping Mode
'D' Total Order Cost	

Relation Name: PRODUCT ORDER and ORDER

Description: Connects the entities PRODUCT ORDER and ORDER

Occurrences: ORDER to PRODUCT ORDER: avg. = 8.5, min. = 1, max. = 200
PRODUCT ORDER to ORDER: avg. = 1, min. = 1, max. = 1

Data Items: 'PK' Order Number
'PK' Product Number

Fig. 3-7. First normal form.

key is not complete. You need to determine which repeating data item(s) need to be added to the primary key in order to cause the other repeating data items to not repeat. This means that the newly created entity has a primary key consisting of:

1. The primary key of the entity from which the data item was removed (Order Number).
2. The data item(s) in the repeating group which causes the others to repeat. For the repeating data items in Fig. 3-6, Product Name or Product Number when added to Order Number cause the other data item to not repeat. From the candidate keys (Order Number + Product Number, and Order Number +

Product Name), the primary key Order Number + Product Number is chosen as the primary key.

3. If a single repeating data item is placed in a new entity, it becomes part of the primary key.

For Fig. 3–6 the new entity is called PRODUCT ORDER. The content of PRODUCT ORDER and ORDER is shown in Fig. 3–7. The new entity (PRODUCT ORDER) is checked for repeating data items based on its primary key. In the new entity there are no repeating data items.

The new entity is connected to the original entity by a relation which identifies that a connection exists between them. This relation consists of the primary key data items of the two entities. In the relation between ORDER and PRODUCT ORDER, the primary key consists of Order Number from the ORDER entity, and Order Number + Product Number from PRODUCT ORDER. Since two of the data items are the same, only one occurrence is listed in the documentation on the relation.

There are three types of relations which can exist: one-to-one, one-to-many, and many-to-many. Fig. 3–7 is an example of a one-to-many relation: an ORDER can have associated with it 0, 1, or many occurrences of PRODUCT ORDER, while PRODUCT ORDER has associated with it 0 or 1 occurrences of ORDER. A one-to-one relation indicates the both entities have 0 or 1 associated occurrences of the other entity. The many-to-many relation indicates 0, 1, or many occurrences of either entity with one occurrence of the other entity.

A relation requires documentation on the number of occurrences one entity can have given one occurrence of the other entity. Given one occurrence of ORDER, how many occurrences of PRODUCT ORDER can occur? The documentation in Fig. 3–7 specifies an average of 8 with a minimum of 1 and a maximum of 200. Given one occurrence of PRODUCT ORDER how many occurrences of ORDER exist? Only one, since the entire primary key of ORDER is contained in PRODUCT ORDER. It is important to specify when the minimum number of occurrences can be zero, because this has a significant impact on the design of the physical data base. For PRODUCT ORDER to ORDER, zero is not allowed, since there must always be an ORDER for a PRODUCT ORDER to exist.

One-to-One Relation. In Appendix A INVOICE and BILL OF LADING stand in a one-to-one relation. When an ORDER is received and filled, a BILL OF LADING and an INVOICE are created. If an ORDER is split and requires two BILLs OF LADING, then two IN-VOICEs are created. There is zero or one INVOICE for a BILL OF LADING, and there is one and only one BILL OF LADING for each INVOICE. In Fig. 3–8, the first example shows the documented one-to-one relation INVOICE and BILL OF LADING.

Many-to-Many Relation. CUSTOMER and SALES REPRESEN-TATIVE is an example of a many-to-many relation found in the Appendix A. Each CUSTOMER can have one or more SALES REP-RESENTATIVEs who handle the account. Each SALES REPRE-SENTATIVE can have one or more CUSTOMERs to service. This results in a many-to-many relation between the two entities. The second example in Fig. 3–8 documents the many-to-many relation CUSTOMER and SALES REPRESENTATIVE.

One-to-One Relation:

Relation Name:	INVOICE and BILL OF LADING
Description:	Connects the entities INVOICE and BILL OF LADING
Occurrences:	INVOICE to BILL OF LADING: avg. = 1, min. = 0, max. = 1
	BILL OF LADING to INVOICE: avg. = 1, min. = 0, max. = 1
Data Items:	'PK' Invoice Number
	'PK' Bill Of Lading Number

Many–to–Many Relation:

Relation Name:	CUSTOMER and SALES REPRESENTATIVE
Description:	Connects the entities CUSTOMER and SALES REPRESEN-TATIVE.
Occurrences:	CUSTOMER to SALES REPRESENTATIVE: avg. = 1, min. = 1, max. = 5
	SALES REPRESENTATIVE to CUSTOMER: avg. = 10, min. = 1, max. = 35
Data Items:	'PK' Customer Number
	'PK' Sales Representative Code

Fig. 3–8. Relation documentation.

A pictorial representation of the entities and their relations is useful in order to maintain the relations between the entities. This picture, called the linkage diagram, is shown in Fig. 3-9. The relations are indicated by lines with arrowheads at the ends. The double arrowhead indicates that zero, one, or more occurrences can exist, the "many" end of the relation. The relation from ORDER to PRODUCT ORDERED is a double arrowhead (many) since the data items contained in PRODUCT ORDER were repeating data items in ORDER. The reverse direction is a single arrowhead, the "one" end of the relation, because the entire primary key of ORDER is contained in the primary key of PRODUCT ORDER.

Second Normal Form

Second normal form makes entities more explicit by verifying that each data item in the entity is uniquely identified by the entity's entire primary key. This is called determining *functional dependency*. If a non–primary key data item is dependent on a subset of the data items composing the primary key, the non–primary key data item must be removed and placed in a new entity. All non–primary key data items must be functionally dependent on the entity's entire primary key to satisfy second normal form.

The table format shown in Fig. 3–10 is used to assist in determining

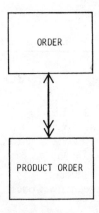

Fig. 3-9. First normal form linkage diagram.

PRODUCT ORDER Table:

	Order Number	Product Number	Order Number + Product Number
Product Name		X	
Product Description		X	
Quantity Ordered			X
Unit Price		X	
'D' Total Product Price			X

ORDER Table:

	Order Number
Customer Name	X
Customer Number	X
Customer Address	X
Shipping Address	X
Shipping Mode	X
'D' Merchandise Total	X
Delivery Charge	X
Order Sales Tax	X
'D' Total Order Cost	X
Order Date	X

Fig. 3–10. Functional dependency table format.

functional dependency. Place the data items composing the primary key and its combinations on the top horizontal row. The non–primary key data items are placed in the left vertical column. If a non–primary key data item is uniquely identified by the primary key data item or combination of primary key data items, mark an X where the two intersect, with only one X per row. Placement of the X is based on discussions with the end-users. Any row in the table that has an X indicates that the data item is functionally dependent on the primary key data items in that column. If the non–primary key data item is functionally dependent on a subset of the primary key, then it is put in a new entity. The new entity's primary key is the subset of the original entity's primary key on which this data item is functionally dependent.

Using Fig. 3-10, Product Description, Product Name, and Unit Price are functionally dependent on a subset of their entity's primary key (Product Number). These data items are placed in a new entity where the data item Product Number, which uniquely identifies them, is the primary key. The entity PRODUCT ORDER is modified by removing the Product Description, Product Name, and Unit Price. The entity ORDER is not changed. The new entity, PRODUCT is checked to ensure that it still satisfies the first normal form rules. If it does not, normalize it to first normal form and then check second normal form again.

A new relation is created connecting PRODUCT ORDER and PRODUCT. This relation has a primary key consisting of Order Number + Product Number from PRODUCT ORDER and Product Number from PRODUCT. Since two of the data items are repeated, only one occurrence is listed in the documentation on the relation. Fig. 3-11 shows the second normal form entities and relations.

Before completing second normal form another rule is checked:

If an entity contains only a primary key and is related to two other entities, then it is not needed.

Such an entity is replaced by a relation which connects the two entities. Our example does not show this condition, but it does occur frequently when one is normalizing data. There are five cases required to show what is done when this occurs. The entities used in Fig. 3-12 will be called X, Y, and Z. Entity Y contains only a primary key and no non-primary key data items.

The expanded Second Normal Form Linkage Diagram for Figure 3-11 is shown in Fig. 3-13.

Third Normal Form

Third normal form checks for transitive dependencies. The definition of a transitive dependency is:

Entity Name:	PRODUCT
Description:	An item produced by the company for sale to customers
Data Items:	'PK' Product Number Product Name
	Product Description Unit Price

Entity Name:	PRODUCT ORDER
Description:	Information on an order for product(s) purchased by a customer
Data Items:	'PK' Order Number Quantity Ordered
	'PK' Product Number 'D' Total Product Price

Entity Name:	ORDER
Description:	A list of items made by our company ordered by a customer
Data Items:	'PK' Order Number Customer Name
	Order Sales Tax Customer Number
	Order Date Customer Address
	Shipping Address 'D' Merchandise Total Cost
	Delivery Charge Shipping Mode
	'D' Total Order Cost

Relation Name:	PRODUCT ORDER and PRODUCT
Description:	Connects the entities PRODUCT ORDER and PRODUCT
Occurrences:	PRODUCT ORDER to PRODUCT: avg. = 1, min. = 1, max. = 1
	PRODUCT to PRODUCT ORDER: avg. = 300, min. = 0, max. = 1500
Data Items:	'PK' Order Number
	'PK' Product Number

Fig. 3-11. Second normal form entity data item lists.

If data item Y is dependent on data item X, and data item Z is dependent on Y, then Z is dependent on X, and Z is said to be *transitively dependent* on X.

Each entity is examined to determine if transitive dependencies exist. In Fig. 3–11 the ORDER entity contains an example of a transitive dependency. Customer Name, Customer Number, Customer Address, and Shipping Address are shown as dependent on Order

In the first case, many-to-one relations connect 'Y' to 'X' and 'Z':

Then the relation between 'X' and 'Z' becomes a "many-to-many".

The second case has one-to-many relations connecting 'Y' to 'X' and 'Z':

Then the relation between 'X' and 'Z' becomes a "many-to-many".

The third case has a many-to-one relation connecting 'Y' to 'X' and a one-to-many relation connecting 'Y' to 'Z':

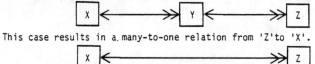

This case results in a. many-to-one relation from 'Z'to 'X'.

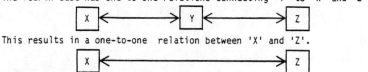

The fourth case has one-to-one relations connecting 'Y' to 'X' and 'Z':

This results in a one-to-one relation between 'X' and 'Z'.

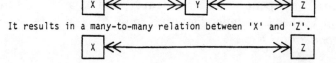

The last case has many-to-many relations connecting 'Y' to 'X' and 'Z':

It results in a many-to-many relation between 'X' and 'Z'.

Fig. 3-12. Resolving entities with only primary key data items.

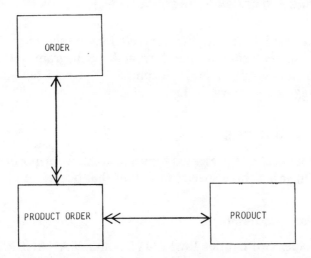

Fig. 3-13. Second normal form linkage diagram.

Number. Customer Name, Customer Address, and Shipping Address are actually dependent on Customer Number and only transitively dependent on Order Number. Based on the definition, Order Number is X, Customer Number is Y, and Customer Name, Customer Address, and Shipping Address are Z.

The data items Customer Name, Customer Number, Customer Address, and Shipping Address are moved to a new entity and a relation is created between the new entity and the ORDER entity. Creating the new entity is done as follows:

1. Transitively dependent items (Customer Name, Customer Number, Customer Address, and Shipping Address), are removed from the original entity.
2. The new entity is created with data item Y (Customer Number) as the primary key and data items Z (Customer Name, Customer Address, and Shipping Address) as non-key data items.
3. A relation is created between the entities which is one in the direction from ORDER to the new entity. Whether it is one or many from the new entity to ORDER needs to be determined. This is done by asking the end-users. In our example it is many.

The revised entities, new entities, and relations are shown in Fig. 3–14.

Expanding the second normal form linkage diagram (Fig. 3–13) to include the new entity creates the completed normalized data model linkage diagram as shown in Fig. 3–15.

SPECIAL SITUATIONS

The previous sections presented typical examples for normalization. However their are three special situations that occur.

Entity Related to Itself

If we consider two entities EMPLOYEE and MANAGER (see Fig. 3–16), with a relation between them defined as:

EMPLOYEE to MANAGER: many-to-one
MANAGER to EMPLOYEE: one-to-many

Entity Name:	ORDER
Description:	A list of items made by our company ordered by a customer
Data Items:	'PK' Order Number Order Sales Tax
	Order Date 'D' Merchandise Total Cost
	Delivery Charge Shipping Mode
	'D' Total Order Cost

Entity Name:	CUSTOMER
Description:	A person or organization which has or could purchase products from our company
Data Items:	'PK' Customer Number Customer Name
	Customer Address Shipping Address

Relation Name:	ORDER and CUSTOMER
Description:	Connects the entities ORDER and CUSTOMER
Occurrences:	ORDER to CUSTOMER: avg. = 1, min. = 1, max. = 1
	CUSTOMER to ORDER: avg. = 2, min. = 0, max. = 20
Data Items:	'PK' Order Number
	'PK' Customer Number

Fig. 3–14. Third normal form.

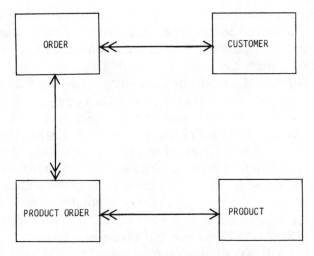

Fig. 3-15. Third normal form linkage diagram.

Entity Name: EMPLOYEE

Description: People who are currently employed by the company.

Data Items: 'PK' Employee Number
Employee Name
Birthdate
Address
Business Location
Business Phone
etc.

Entity Name: MANAGER

Description: A person who has subordinates reporting to them or a Manager in a staff position.

Data Items: 'PK' Manager Number
Manager Name
Birthdate
Address
Business Location
Business Phone
etc.

Fig. 3-16. Special situation 1, entity-data list.

Since they contain some of the same data items, they must be reviewed with the end-user to determine if they are the homonyms. If they are, they are combined. If not, the common data items such as Address or Business Location must be qualified, generally with the name of the entity. This must be done since a non-key data item can not be contained in more than one normalized entity.

Evaluating these entities with the end-user indicated that all MANAGERs are EMPLOYEEs, but not all EMPLOYEEs are MANAGERs. This is represented by making the data item Manager Number a synonym for Employee Number. Then the MANAGER entity is combined with EMPLOYEE by making each data item in MANAGER a synonym for its corresponding data item in EMPLOYEE or by adding it to EMPLOYEE. The relation MANAGER to EMPLOYEE remains but becomes a relation from EMPLOYEE to EMPLOYEE. On the Normalized Data Model's Linkage Diagram this is represented by labeling the relation as shown in Fig. 3-17.

For the primary key of the relation, use the Manager Number (a synonym for Employee Number) in addition to Employee Number to clarify that the relation is between the Employee and the subset called Manager (see Fig. 3-18).

Non-Primary Key Data Items in Two Entities

This situation is similar to the entity related to itself. Here, not all INSTRUCTORs are STUDENTs (where, in the other situation, all MANAGERS were EMPLOYEEs), and also most STUDENTs are not INSTRUCTORs, so that the two entities cannot be combined. Their entity-data lists are shown in Fig. 3-19. Because non-primary

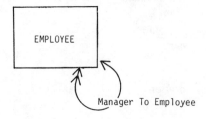

Fig. 3-17. Special situation 1, linkage diagram (revised).

Relation Name: MANAGER and EMPLOYEE

Description: Connects the entities EMPLOYEE and EMPLOYEE

Occurrences: EMPLOYEE to MANAGER: avg. = 1, min. = 0, max. = 1
MANAGER to EMPLOYEE: avg. = 9, min. = 0, max. = 125

Data Items: 'PK' <u>Employee Number</u>
'PK' <u>Manager Number</u>

Fig. 3-18. Special situation 1, relation.

key data items can not be contained in two entities, data items such as Address and Birthdate must be qualified. This results in a revised entity–data item list in Fig. 3–20. This causes some data redundancy, but it accurately reflects the user environment.

Multiple Relations Between Entities

There are cases where more than one relation exists between two entities. When this occurs, each relation is labeled and documented. In Appendix A, the CUSTOMER entity has two relations to CUSTOMER ADDRESS. One is a BILL TO relation and the other is

Entity Name: STUDENT

Description: A person attending courses at the college

Data Items: 'PK' <u>Student Number</u>
<u>Student Name</u>
Address
Birthdate
etc.

Entity Name: INSTRUCTOR

Description: A person who teaches a course

Data Items: 'PK' <u>Instructor Number</u>
<u>Instructor Name</u>
Address
Birthdate
etc.

Fig. 3-19. STUDENT and INSTRUCTOR entity–data item lists.

Entity Name: STUDENT

Description: A person attending courses at the college

Data Items: 'PK' <u>Student Number</u>
              <u>Student Name</u>
              Student Address
              Student Birthdate
              etc.

Entity Name: INSTRUCTOR

Description: A person who teaches a course

Data Items: 'PK' <u>Instructor Number</u>
              <u>Instructor Name</u>
              Instructor Address
              Instructor Birthdate
              etc.

Fig. 3-20. Revised STUDENT and INSTRUCTOR entity-data item lists.

a SHIP TO. These relations exist because a CUSTOMER ADDRESS can be either a Ship To address or a Bill To address or both. To minimize data redundancy, one entity is created for CUSTOMER ADDRESS and two relations are created. This allows different CUSTOMER subsidiaries to have the same Billing Address or Shipping Address because they have common billing or common shipment receiving locations. The data item Customer Number is defined in Fig. 3-21, while Fig. 3-22 specifies the content for the SHIP TO and BILL TO relations, and the entity CUSTOMER.

Data Item: Customer Number

Description: A descriptive code identifying a Customer and its sub-
                    sidiaries. The first 3 characters identify the parent com-
                    pany and the last 4 identify the subsidiary. If there are no
                    subsidiaries the last 4 characters are "000A".

Standard Value Set: 7 characters, AAN-NNNA

Composed of: Parent Company Number
                    Subsidiary Number

Fig. 3-21. Customer number definition.

Entity Name: CUSTOMER

Description: A person or business who has or may purchase PRODUCTS

Data items:
'PK' Customer Number
Customer Name
Credit Rating
Account Status
etc.

Entity Name: CUSTOMER ADDRESS

Description: The billing or shipping locations for a CUSTOMER

Data Items:
'PK' Parent Company Number
'PK' Customer Street Address
'PK' Zip Code
City Name
etc.

Relation Name: SHIP TO ADDRESS

Description: Connects the entities CUSTOMER and CUSTOMER ADDRESS, indicating the address a Customer's order is sent.
NOTE: Parent Company Number is part of Customer Number data item.

Occurrences: CUSTOMER to CUSTOMER ADDRESS: avg. = 1, min. = 1, max. = 3
CUSTOMER ADDRESS to CUSTOMER: avg. = 1.3, min. = 1, max. = 15

Data Items: 'PK' Customer Number   'PK' Customer Street Address
'PK' Zip Code

Relation Name: BILL TO ADDRESS

Description: Connects the entities CUSTOMER and CUSTOMER ADDRESS indicating the address a Customer's bill is sent.
NOTE: Parent Company Number is part of Customer Number data item.

Occurrences: CUSTOMER to CUSTOMER ADDRESS: avg. = 1, min. = 1, max. = 1
CUSTOMER ADDRESS to CUSTOMER: avg. = 2, min. = 1, max. = 28

Data-items: 'PK' Customer Number   'PK' Customer Street Address
'PK' Zip Code

Fig. 3-22. CUSTOMER entity and relation descriptions.

4. USAGE DATA MODEL

INTRODUCTION

The Usage Data Model collects information on current and future uses of data. The usage information includes the end-user's perspective on how data are used, how often they are used, and entity and relation volume statistics. Since the physical data base is designed from the normalized data model, the usage data model identifies the subset required by a system and ensures that it is performance tuned to satisfy the end-user's needs. In normalization there were no constraints imposed by the volume of or activity on data. For physical data base design, knowledge of the volume and access activity is required in order to merge end-user needs with current computer technology.

The usage data model defines data accesses and identifies the normalized entities and relations required by the access. It cross-references activity on entities and relations and identifies their volume estimates. In order to develop flexible data bases, look at current and known future uses for data when developing the model. This is critical to a data base developed in phases and is planned for direct use by many systems. The physical data base design should be flexible enough to meet unknown usages with minimal change. This is accomplished if the usage data model is broad enough in scope so the physical data base is tuned to satisfy current and future information requirements.

All processes within the business functions need not be analyzed when developing the model. Data base tuning decisions can be made based on a subset of the business functions' processes. Approximately 20 percent of the business processes will yield about 80 percent of the access activity. This 20 percent defines the *critical business processes*

(CBP). They must be chosen carefully to provide an overall view of data usage based on high activity and how critical it is to the business. Within each business function are processes, activities, and information requirements from which the usage information is obtained. The following information is collected to document the usage data model:

1. Volume estimates
2. Access statements
3. Cross-reference access-critical activities and entities
4. Entity usage and derivable data

VOLUME ESTIMATES

The usage data model's volume estimates identify the number of occurrences for each entity and relation in the normalized data model. These estimates are used to determine the data's physical storage requirements and structures, and identify potential data access problems. Two sets of estimates are required: entity occurrences and relation occurrences.

Entity Occurrences

Entity occurrences are determined by estimating the number of occurrences of each entity in the normalized data model or from information documented in other systems. There are expressed as an average or a maximum and minimum if there is a wide variance in the number of possible occurrence. Expected yearly growth is documented as a percent of the average volume. Document entity occurrences as shown in Table 4–1.

Relation Occurrences

The second set of volume estimates is for relation occurrences. Determine for each relation in the normalized data model the average number of occurrences for each entity the relation connects. To determine this, ask: How many occurrences of each entity will most frequently be found given one occurrence of the other entity. Docu-

Table 4-1. Entity Occurrences.

ENTITY	AVERAGE VOLUME	MINIMUM VOLUME	MAXIMUM VOLUME	YEARLY GROWTH
BILL OF LADING	22,000	8,000	40,000	7.0%
BILL OF LADING—FREIGHT	170,000	—	—	7.0%
CARRIER	500	—	—	1.0%
CARRIER—GEOGRAPHIC LOCATION	4,500	—	—	2.0%
CUSTOMER	8,500	—	—	10.0%
CUSTOMER ADDRESS	11,400	—	—	8.5%
FREIGHT	11	—	—	0.0%
GEOGRAPHIC LOCATION	900	—	—	0.0%
INVOICE	23,000	—	40,000	7.0%
ORDER	21,000	—	35,000	7.0%
ORDER—PRODUCT LINE	150,000	—	—	3.0%
PRODUCT	3,000	—	—	3.0%
PRODUCT—BILL OF LADING	185,000	—	420,000	7.5%
PRODUCT LINE	186	—	—	1.5%
PRODUCT ORDER	400,000	—	890,000	7.0%
PRODUCT—WAREHOUSE	75,000	1,000	150,000	3.5%
REGION	16	—	—	0.0%
RETURN/CREDIT	1,600	1,200	3,200	−0.5%
RETURN/CREDIT—PRODUCT	8,000	—	—	−0.5%
SALES REPRESENTATIVE	1,200	—	—	2.5%
WAREHOUSE	50	—	—	0.1%

ment the results in the format of Table 4–2. List the entities across the top and down the left column. If there is no relation between two normalized entities (based on the normalized data model), then 'NR' (No Relation), is entered in the table. For each relation that exists, enter the average number of occurrences for the entities it connects. For each entity there may be zero, one, or multiple occurrences given one occurrence of the entity to which it is related. If there is a wide range of occurrences, specify a maximum and minimum.

Using the normalized data model's linkage diagram from Appendix A, Table 4–2 represents a subset of its relation volumes. The number of occurrences were obtained from interviews with end-users and from evaluating data in existing information systems. Table 4–2 shows the following information for the ORDER entity:

- ORDER is not related to BILL OF LADING–FREIGHT or CARRIER–GEOGRAPHIC LOCATION.

Table 4-2. Relation Occurrences Report.

TO ENTITY→ FROM ENTITY	BILL OF LADING	BILL OF LADING-FREIGHT	CARRIER	CARRIER-GEO LOCATION	CUSTOMER
BILL OF LADING	—[1]	7[2]	1.1[3]	NR	NR
BILL OF LADING-FREIGHT	1	NR	NR	NR	NR
CARRIER	—[4]	NR	NR	9[5]	NR
CARRIER-GEOGRAPHIC LOCATION	NR	NR	1	NR	NR
CUSTOMER	NR	NR	NR	NR	NR
CUSTOMER ADDRESS (SHIP TO)	NR	NR	NR	NR	1.1[6]
CUSTOMER ADDRESS (BILL TO)	NR	NR	NR	NR	1.8[7]
FREIGHT	NR	1,500[8]	NR	NR	NR
GEOGRAPHIC LOCATION	NR	NR	NR	4	NR
INVOICE	1	NR	NR	NR	NR
ORDER	1.3*	NR	1*	NR	1
ORDER-PRODUCT LINE	NR	NR	NR	NR	NR
PRODUCT	NR	NR	NR	NR	NR
PRODUCT-BILL OF LADING	1	NR	NR	NR	NR
PRODUCT LINE	NR	NR	NR	NR	20,000[9]
PRODUCT ORDER	NR	NR	NR	NR	NR
PRODUCT-WAREHOUSE	NR	NR	NR	NR	NR
REGION	NR	NR	NR	NR	NR
RETURN/CREDIT	NR	NR	NR	NR	1*
RETURN/CREDIT-PRODUCT	1	NR	NR	NR	NR

* Can be zero	[1] Range 1–35
[2] Maximum 11	[3] Range 1–5
[4] Range 0–500	[5] Range 1–210
[6] Range 1–21	[7] Range 1–8
[8] Maximum 22,000	[9] Maximum 30,000

- For an ORDER there are an average of 1.3 occurrences of BILL OF LADING. The asterisk (*) indicates that an ORDER may not have an associated BILL OF LADING.
- Each ORDER can have a specific CARRIER requested by a Customer. This is shown by the occurrence of 1 followed by an asterisk(*). The asterisk (*) indicates there are occurrences of an ORDER where no CARRIER assigned.
- For an ORDER there is always 1 occurrence of CUSTOMER.

As shown in the Table 4–2, unique situations are documented at the bottom of the table as footnotes. They are used if the number of occurrences is a range, can be zero, or for unusual distributions. For example, the average occurrences of the entity CARRIER to the entity CARRIER–GEOGRAPHIC LOCATION is 9 with a range of 1–210.

ACCESS INFORMATION

Critical Business Processes

Not all business functions are required to obtain usage information for physical data base tuning. Review each business function to determine the critical business processes (CBP). During this review identify the data requirements for each CBP identified. Critical business processes have one or more of the following characteristics:

- A high data access rate. This occurs when a process has many data items accessed or has many accesses against the data base.
- A high function occurrence rate. This indicates the number of times the function is initiated per interval of time.
- Importance to the user. There are processes that are higher priority relative to other processes. These are identified so the physical designer can take them into consideration when designing the physical data base.

These CBPs provide sufficient data for designing the physical data base.

When applying the data models to a specific system, the choice of CBPs is done as early as possible in system analysis. Selection cannot be made randomly. It must be made carefully to yield a representative sample of data usage such that approximately 80% of the data base accesses are represented, the various types of data base access activity are included, and each of the probable system environments (batch, on-line, etc) are included. An example of a list of CBPs is shown in Fig. 4–1.

Access Statements

Access statements for each critical business process profile the access against the data. For each activity, document the business function and process it supports, and the activity occurrence rate. The activity

ACTIVITY NAME	PROCESS NAME	BUSINESS FUNCTION
GENERATE INVOICES	BILLING	ACCOUNTING
GENERATE BACK-ORDERS		
DETERMINE ORDER STATUS	CUSTOMER SERVICE	SALES

Fig. 4-1. Critical business process list.

occurrence rate specifies the number of times the given activity is initiated per interval of time. Fig. 4-2 shows the documentation format. For an activity, one or more sets of access statements may be needed. Different actions on the same grouping of data or the same action on different groupings of data requires multiple sets of data requirements. These provide a profile of the data accesses made by the function. These accesses are documented in access requirement statements, as shown in Fig. 4-3. The components of the access requirement statements are defined as follows:

ADD, REMOVE, MODIFY, and RETRIEVE identify the action to be performed on the data contained in the data list.

ADD	New values for the data list are added.
REMOVE	Existing values for the data list are deleted.
MODIFY	Existing values for the data list are changed.
RETRIEVE	Existing values for the data list are extracted.
Data Item List	Specifies the names of the data items retrieved from or entered into the data base, based on the Action.
Specific Values	Specifies that specific value(s) are given or the access data item(s).
Range of Values	Specifies maximum and minimum values are given for at least one access data item. The access is for all values between and including the maximum and minimum.
All Values	Specifies that no specific value is given for one or more of the access data items. The access is for all occurrences of the entry data items(s).

Business Function:	Sales
Process:	Customer Service
Activity:	Determine Order Status
Activity Occurrence Rate:	Daily

Fig. 4-2. Access requirement's activity information.

ADD			Specific Values		
REMOVE	Data	FOR	Range of Values	OF	Access Data Item(s)
MODIFY	List		All Values		
RETRIEVE					

HAPPENS	number	TIMES PER PROCESS OCCURRENCE

Fig. 4-3. Access statement.

Access Data Item(s)   The data item(s) used to access the data base to add, remove, modify, or retrieve the data specified in the data item list. They represent the data items the end-user would use to ask for the data item list.

An example of an access statement is shown in Fig. 4-4.

CROSS REFERENCE ACCESS STATEMENTS AND ENTITIES

Once access statements are identified, they need to be related to the entities in the normalized data model. Since access statements are specified in terms of data items, the entities and relations containing the data items need to be specified for physical data base design. This acts as a check and balance to ensure the data specified in this data model is included in the normalized data model.

Take each access statement and determine the entities which contain the data specified in the Data List and determine the Entry Entities. This results in logical access paths which illustrate the logical

Business Function:	Sales	
Process:	Customer Service	
Activity:	Determine Order Status	
Activity Occurrence Rate:	Daily	

RETRIEVE	Bill Of Lading Number	FOR	Range Of Values	OF	Order Request
	Order Number				Date
	Total Order Cost				Shipping Date
	Order Date				

HAPPENS	3	TIMES PER PROCESS OCCURRENCE

Fig. 4-4. Documented access statement.

sequence in which the data is acted upon. Two steps are required to define each access statement's logical access Path(s):

- Determine entry entity(s)
- Determine entity(s) accessed

An Entry Entity is defined as the entity or entities which contain the Access Data Item(s) specified by a Access Statement. Two rules are followed in determining Entry Entities. For these rules, use the entity–data item list of Appendix A and the specified figure.

Rule 1. Single Access Data Item

1.1. If the access data item is a non–primary key data item, there is only one entity which can contain it. This is because the rules of normalization state that a non–primary key data item can not be contained in more than one normalized entity. The access data item in Fig. 4–5 is a non–primary key data item which only exists in the PRODUCT ORDER entity. Therefore, the entry entity is PRODUCT ORDER.

1.2. If the access data item is a primary key data item, more than one entry entity can be found. The entry entity is the one which contains only that data item as its primary key. In Fig. 4–6, Order Number is the access data item which is contained in the PRODUCT, PRODUCT ORDER, and ORDER-PRODUCT LINE entities because it is part of their primary key. Since it is the entire primary key of ORDER and only part of the other two entities' primary keys, the ORDER entity is the entry entity. When an en-

---

RETRIEVE Product Number   FOR Range of Values OF Order Date
            Quantity Ordered
            Total Product Price
HAPPENS 2 TIMES PER PROCESS OCCURRENCE
The only possible entry entity is PRODUCT ORDER.

Fig. 4–5. Non-primary key access data items (rule 1.1).

RETRIEVE Product Number   FOR Specific Values OF Order Number
          Quantity Ordered
          Customer Number
          Customer Name
          Customer Address (Bill To)
          Order Date
          Shipping Date
          Shipping Mode

HAPPENS 88 TIMES PER PROCESS OCCURRENCE

Possible entry entities: ORDER, ORDER-PRODUCT LINE, and PRODUCT
ORDER

Using Rule 1.2, ORDER is the entry entity.

Fig. 4-6. Single primary key access data item (rule 1.2).

tity cannot be found which contains the access data item as the
only data item as its primary key, select the entity which also contains data items listed in the access statement's data list.

Rule 2. Multiple Access Data Items

When there is more than one access data item, compare the access
data items to the normalized data model's entity-data item list.
Each access data item is either a non-primary key data item in an
entity or contained in the primary key of one or more entities.

Three situations occur:

2.1. If all access data items are non-primary key data items then all
     entities identified are entry entities. Fig. 4-7 has two non-pri-
     mary key access data items. Because they are non-primary key
     data items, each one can only be contained in one entity. There-
     fore ORDER and PRODUCT ORDER are the entry entities.
2.2. If all access data items are primary key data items, select entry
     entities as follows:
     Is there an entity whose primary key is composed of all the
     access data items? *If yes,* it is the entry entity. *If no,* select the

RETRIEVE Bill of Lading Number FOR Range of Values OF Shipping Date
            Order Number   Order Request Date
            Total Order Cost
            Order Date

HAPPENS   3   TIMES PER PROCESS OCCURRENCE

The entry entities are ORDER and PRODUCT ORDER

Fig. 4–7. Multiple non-primary key access data items (rule 2.1).

entities in which each access data item is the only data item used as the primary key.

The access statement in Fig. 4–8 has two access data items which are both primary key data items. A total of five entities contain one or both of these access data items. However, only PRODUCT-WAREHOUSE contains both in its primary key. Based on rule 2.2, this is the entry entity.

2.3. If the access data items are a combination of non–primary key and primary key data items, the entities containing non–primary key data items are entry entities, while the primary key data items are evaluated as in part 2 of the rule. In Fig. 4–9, one access data item, Product Number, is contained in the primary key of five entities and the other, shipping date year, is a non–primary key data item contained in the PRODUCT ORDER entity. Since Product Number is also contained in the PRODUCT ORDER

MODIFY Quantity on Hand FOR Specific Values OF Product Number
                                                Warehouse Number

HAPPENS 10,000 TIMES PER PROCESS OCCURRENCE

Possible entry entities: PRODUCT, PRODUCT ORDER, PRODUCT-BILL OF LADING, PRODUCT-WAREHOUSE, and WARE-HOUSE.

Using Rule 2.2, PRODUCT-WAREHOUSE is the entry entity.

Fig. 4–8. Multiple primary key access data items (rule 2.2).

RETRIEVE Quantity Shipped   FOR Specific Values OF Product Number
          Customer Name   Shipping Date Year
          Geographic Location
          Code

HAPPENS 3,000 TIMES PER PROCESS OCCURRENCE

Possible entry entities: PRODUCT, PRODUCT ORDER, PRODUCT-BILL OF
                          LADING, PRODUCT-WAREHOUSE, and WARE-
                          HOUSE.

Using Rule 2.3, PRODUCT ORDER is the entry entity.

Fig. 4-9. Multiple primary key and non-primary key access data items (rule 2.3).

entity, PRODUCT ORDER is selected as the only entry entity. If Product Number was not contained in the same entity, then there would have been two entry entities. The selection of which of the five follows rule 2.2.

To identify entities required to satisfy the access statements data list, compare the data list to the normalized data model's entity-data item list. Select the entities which contain the data in the data list. For data items contained in a primary key more than one entity may be found. Select the entity which contains the data item as the only data item in the primary key. When this can not be done, select from the entities identified the entity which contains the most other data from the data list. If that fails, select the entity related to one of the other entities selected or related to the entry entity(s).

For non-primary key data items, only one entity will be found.

For each access statement the entity (or entities) selected, the data items accessed, and the data item(s) used as access data item(s) are documented as shown in Fig. 4-10. In addition the Access Mode to each entity required by the access statement is identified. The access Mode identifies whether the entity is accessed by data item(s) or a relation. For each entity specify one of the following access modes:

Full key   All entry primary key data items are access data
              items.

```
Business Function:        Sales
Process:                  Customer Service
Activity:                 Determine Order Status
Activity Occurrence Rate: Daily
```

```
RETRIEVE  Bill Of Lading Number FOR Range Of Values OF  Order Request Date
          Order Number                                  Shipping Date
          Total Order Cost
          Order Date

HAPPENS  3  TIMES-PER PROCESS OCCURRENCE
```

ENTITY	DATA LIST DATA ITEMS	ACCESS DATA ITEM	ACCESS MODE
ORDER	Order Number Total Order Cost Order Date	Order Request Date	non-key
BILL OF LADING	Bill Of Lading Number	Shipping Date	non-key

Fig. 4-10. Access statement documentation.

Partial key	At least one but not all the primary key data items are specified as access data items.
Non-Key	Access to the entity is by non-primary key data items.
(blank)	Access to the entity is through a relation connecting it to another entity.

ENTITY USAGE

An entity usage report is created to specify for each entity the processes which access it, the access mode and activity occurrence rate. This aids the data base administrator in physical data base design, and reduces maintenance work when evaluating the impact of a change to the data base. In physical data base design each entity becomes a seg-

Entity Name: ORDER		Date: 5/4/8x
		Issue: 1
Activity Name	Access Mode	Activity Occurrence Rate
Generate Invoices Determine Order Status etc.	Non-key	Daily Hourly

Fig. 4-11. Entity usage report.

ment (repeating group). When data changes, the entity is identified and the processes impacted are easily identified. A sample report format is shown in Fig. 4-11.

DERIVABLE DATA

During physical data base design the designer determines whether to store or derive derivable data. The derivable data report lists processes accessing derivable data and documents the activity's occurrence rate. This list includes processes which access the data item(s) used to derive the derivable data item. The report format shown in Fig. 4-12 provides the data base administrator with information required to determine whether to store or derive the derivable data.

CONCLUSION

The purpose of the Usage Data Model is to tune the physical data base for performance when necessary. The amount of tuning depends on the data base management system used to implement the physical data base design. When doing the usage data model for a data planning project, the usage data model is limited to the entity volumes, relation volumes, and access information for the business function's primary input documents. All other usage requirements and the detailed usage information is collected during development of systems which support

Derivable Data Item:	Total Order Dollars	Date:	5/4/8x	
Component Data Items(s):	Unit Price	Issue:	1	
Quantity Ordered	Delivery Charge			
Order Sales Tax		Activity Occurrence Rate	Access Occurrence Rate	
Retrieving Processes/Activities:				

Customer Service
  Determine Shipments Made
  Determine Order Status
		Weekly
		Daily
			3
			3	

Updating Processes/Activities:				
Change Order Information		Daily	20	

Fig. 4-12. Derivable data report.

the business function(s) for which the data planning data models were built. During these systems' system analysis, the data models are validated, details are added, and performance considerations are applied when necessary.

5. STRUCTURAL DATA MODEL

INTRODUCTION

Conversion of a normalized data model to the a set of logical data structures which can be implemented by a data base management system (DBMS) is done in the structural data model. By manipulating the normalized data model's linkage diagram, logical data structures are produced. Creating this model is dependent on specific interpretations of the relations in the linkage diagram. Before beginning a few terms need to be defined:

Child entity   The entity at the many end of a one-to-many relation is called the *child*. Fig. 5–1 shows entity B as a child of entity A.

Parent entity   The entity at the one end of a one-to-many relation is called the *parent*. In Fig. 5–1 entity A is the parent of B.

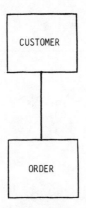

Fig. 5-1. Child and parent entity example.

Path   A path is a set of two or more entities which are connected by relations.

Direct Path   A one-to-many or one-to-one relation which connects two entities.

Indirect Path   An indirect path is a path which connects two entities by using two or more one-to-many or one-to-one relations. The flow of the indirect path is in the one-to-many direction.

Appendix A contains a completed normalized data model and the structural data models for hierarchical, network, and relational data base management systems.

Hierarchical/Network DBMS Logical Data Structure

Seven steps are required to develop the structural data model for a hierarchical DBMS while a network DBMS requires the first four and the seventh steps:

1. Resolve implied relations
2. Modify many-to-many relations
3. Modify identity relations
4. Identify potentially redundant entities
5. Identify roots
6. Identify the pseudo-roots
7. Develop the logical data structures

Resolve Implied Relations. An implied relation exists when a path between two entities can be implied by following an indirect path connecting the same two entities. For each implied relation, answer the following question:

Will the same data be obtained if the indirect path is used instead of the direct path?

If the answer is yes, the paths are redundant and the direct path is removed. If the answer is no, the direct path is not removed.

Modify Many-to-Many Relations. A many-to-many relation is a relation between two entities in which a given occurrence of each entity will be related to zero, one, or more than one occurrence of the entity to which it is related. Many-to-many relations are removed in order to utilize many of today's DBMSs. Each many-to-many relation is examined and eliminated for hierarchical DBMSs and for network DBMSs they are eliminated when possible. When all have been examined and modified, the modified linkage diagram contains one-to-many and one-to-one relations. A many-to-many relation is resolved by finding a common child, finding a common parent, or creating a pseudo-child.

Modify Identity Relations. An identity is a relation between two entities which contains a simple (one-to-one) relation. Identities are modified so valid logical data structures can be drawn. The logical data structure implies a parent–child relation while the identity implies equal or parent-to-parent relation. The choice of one entity subordinate to the other is not to be made at this point. It is resolved during physical data base design, using information provided in the usage data model.

Identify Potentially Redundant Entities. An entity which has more than one complex ("many") relation entering it is potentially redundant. It is potentially redundant because it is subordinate to (the child of) multiple entities. These entities are marked to remind the designer that a placement decision must be made when designing the physical data base.

Identify Roots. A root is an entity which is the top of a logical data structure. An entity is a root if only simple relations enter it or if no relations enter it. It becomes the starting point for the logical data structures.

Identify Pseudo-Roots. A pseudo-root is a redundant entity which has one or more simple relations (the "one" end of a relation) entering it. It is identified as a pseudo-root to avoid duplicating the dependent entities in each logical data structure where it occurs. To determine the placement of pseudo-roots in the physical data base, use the DBMS modeling tools and the usage information from the usage data model.

Develop the Logical Data Structures. Two approaches to drawing the logical structures are defined because of differing physical data base implementation techniques required by hierarchical and network DBMSs. Other data base management systems' structures will require their own approach to developing their logical data structure.

Relational DBMS

For a Relational DBMS three steps are required to produce the table definitions:

1. Resolve identity relations
2. Resolve one-to-many relations
3. Resolve many-to-many relations

Resolve Identity Relations. An identity (one-to-one) relation is removed by taking the primary key data item(s) from each entity and placing them in the other's entity–data item list.

Resolve One-to-Many Relations. One-to-many relations are removed by taking the primary key of the entity at the one (single arrowhead) end of the relation and placing it in the entity–data item list of the entity at the many (double arrowhead) end of the relation.

Resolve Many-to-Many Relations. Many-to-many relations are handled the same as for hierarchical/network DBMSs. If a common child or common parent cannot satisfy the many-to-many, a pseudo-child entity is created.

DEVELOPMENT OF THE HIERARCHICAL/NETWORK STRUCTURAL DATA MODEL

Creating the structural data model will transform the normalized data model to a parent–child or relational structure. No arrows are required in the logical data structures because the parent–child relation represents a one-to-many relation with the many going down. One or more logical data structures are drawn for a linkage diagram using this concept. As each step of the structural data model is performed, a copy of the normalized data model's linkage diagram is modified.

Development of the structural data model does not actually change the normalized data model's linkage diagram. Fig. 5-2 is a nonspecific example which shows the steps required to transform a normalized data model to a logical data structure. Fig. 5-3 uses a subset of the

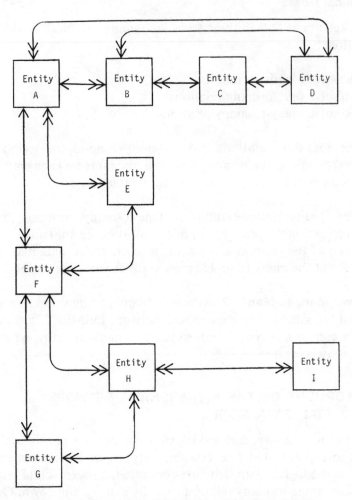

Fig. 5-2. Sample normalized data model linkage diagram.

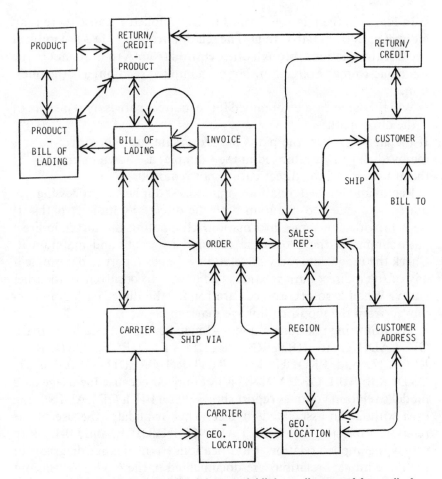

Fig. 5-3. Subset of the normalized data model linkage diagram of Appendix A.

documentation example in Appendix A to show an example of the transformation.

Resolve Implied Relations (Step 1)

An implied relation exists when a direct path between two entities can be implied by following an indirect path connecting the same two entities.

In Fig. 5–2, the relation from B to D is implied because there is an indirect path from B to C to D. The relation from A to D is not implied because the relations through other entities from A to D are not in the same one-to-many direction. For each implied relation, ask the question:

Will the same data be obtained if the indirect path is used instead of the direct path?

If the answer is yes, the paths are redundant and the direct path is removed. B to D is removed in the example, as shown in Fig. 5–4. If the answer is no, the direct path is not removed.

Removing implied relations minimizes duplicate processing required to create and maintain both the direct and indirect paths. If both provide the same information, eliminating the direct indirect path eliminates the processing required to create and maintain it. Check the usage data model's relation volumes report to determine if any of the indirect path relations can have zero occurrences to either entity. When zero occurrences are found, the direct path is not removed from the modified linkage diagram.

The following relations in Fig. 5–3 may be implied relations: BILL OF LADING to RETURN/CREDIT—PROJECT, ORDER to REGION, and PRODUCT to RETURN/CREDIT—PRODUCT. ORDER to BILL OF LADING is not implied because the usage data model's relation volumes report shows that a BILL OF LADING can exist without an associated Invoice. This invalidates the use of the relation connecting BILL OF LADING, INVOICE, and ORDER to satisfy the implied relation. Modifications to the linkage diagram for the three implied relations are documented in the modified relations report which specifies how a relation was changed. The modified relation report and modified linkage diagram for the revisions to Fig. 5–3 are shown in Figs. 5–5(a) and 5–5(b).

Modify Many-to-Many Relations (Step 2)

Many-to-many relations are modified to effectively utilize today's nonrelational data base management systems (DBMSs). Each many-to-many relation is examined and eliminated for hierarchical DMBSs. For network DBMSs they are eliminated when possible.

Many-to-many relations are analyzed using the techniques in the

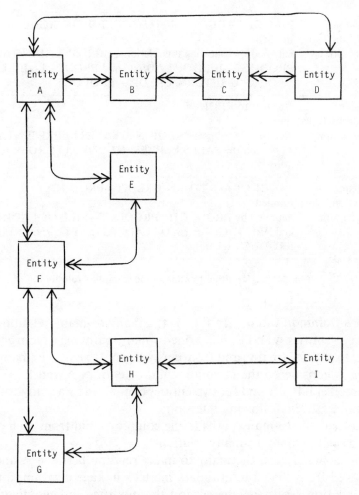

Fig. 5-4. Sample modified linkage diagram: implied relations.

order shown below. If one method fails, try the next one until it is resolved.

1. Find a common child
2. Find a common parent
3. Create a pseudo-child (for hierarchical DBMSs)

Relation:	BILL OF LADING to RETURN/CREDIT—PRODUCT
Relation Type:	Implied
Description:	Satisfied by following the relations: BILL OF LADING to PRODUCT—BILL OF LADING and PRODUCT—BILL OF LADING to RETURN/CREDIT—PRODUCT
Relation:	ORDER to REGION
Relation Type:	Implied
Description:	Satisfied by using the REGION to SALES REPRESENTA-TIVE and the SALES REPRESENTATIVE to ORDER relations.
Relation:	PRODUCT to RETURN/CREDIT—PRODUCT
Relation Type:	Implied
Description:	Satisfied by PRODUCTto PRODUCT—BILL OF LADING and PRODUCT—BILL OF LADING to RETURN/CREDIT—PRODUCT relations

Fig. 5-5(a). Modified relations report: implied relations.

Find a Common Child. In Fig. 5-4, a many-to-many relation exists between entities A and E. Since one-to-many paths exist from entity A (one) to entity F (many) and from entity E (one) to entity F (many), entity F is considered the common child of entities A and E. When a common child, is found for two entities connected by a many-to-many relation, ask the following question:

Can the one-to-many paths to the common child from each parent replace the many-to-many relation?

If the answer is yes, the many-to-many relation between A and E is removed from the structural data model's linkage diagram, a modified relation report is created and the modified linkage diagram is changed, as shown in Fig. 5-6. If the answer is no, the structural data Model's Linkage Diagram remains the same and finding a common parent is examined.

Find a Common Parent. In Fig. 5-4, a many-to-many relation exists between entities G and H. A one-to-many path exists from entity F to G entity and from entity F to entity H which causes entity F to be considered the common parent of entities G and H. When a common parent is found, ask the following question:

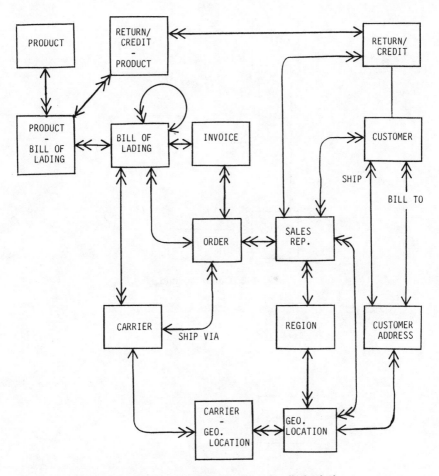

Fig. 5-5(b). Modified linkage diagram: implied relations.

Can the paths from the common parent to each child replace the many-to-many relation?

If the answer is no, leave the linkage diagram as is and resolve it by creating a pseudo-child. If the answer is yes, the relation between G and H is removed from the structural data model's linkage diagram. The modified linkage diagram is shown in Fig. 5-7.

Hierarchical DBMS. For most hierarchical data base management systems a pseudo-child is created when a common parent or common

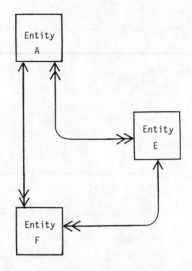

Fig. 5-6. Common child.

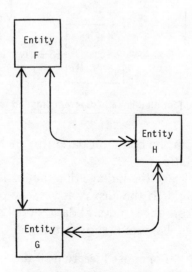

Fig. 5-7. Common parent.

child are not found or are not valid for a many-to-many relation. The pseudo-child is created as follows:

1. Create a child entity between the two entities. This entity contains the primary key data items from the two entities connected by the many-to-many relation.
2. Label the pseudo-child entity with a combination of both entities' names separated by a dash.
3. Create a one-to-many relation from each entity to the pseudo-child—one into the original entity and many into the pseudo-child entity.
4. Use the primary keys of the two connected entities as the primary key of the pseudo-child entity.

Figure 5-4 has a many-to-many relation between entities H and I which can only be solved by a pseudo-child. After modifying the many-to-many relation using the pseudo-child rules, it is redrawn as shown in Fig. 5-8.

Figure 5-9 shows Fig. 5-4 with its many-to-many relations resolved for hierarchical data base management systems.

Figure 5-5 has three many-to-many relations: BILL OF LADING to CARRIER, GEOGRAPHIC LOCATION to SALES REPRE-SENTATIVE, and SALES REPRESENTATIVE to CUSTOMER. BILL OF LADING to CARRIER does not have a common child or a common parent, therefore a pseudo-child is created. GEOGRAPHIC LOCATION to SALES REPRESENTATIVE does not have a common child but does have a common parent. Its many-to-many relation is removed from the linkage diagram.

The common parent or common child is evaluated to determine if it will always provide the same data provided by the many-to-many rela-

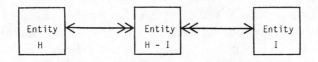

Entity 'H-I' is the pseudo-child entity.

Fig. 5-8. Pseudo-child.

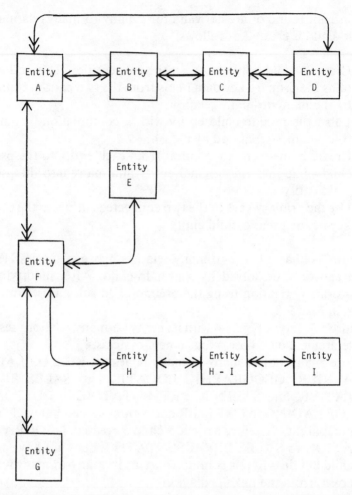

Fig. 5-9. Sample modified linkage diagram: resolved many-to-many relations.

tion. Since every GEOGRAPHIC LOCATION is always contained within one REGION and every SALES REPRESENTATIVE is assigned to one and only one REGION, the common parent REGION allows us to drop the many-to-many relation between GEOGRAPHIC LOCATION and SALES REPRESENTATIVE. If either of the relations to the common parent could be zero, the common parent would not be valid.

The many-to-many relation SALES REPRESENTATIVE to CUS-TOMER cannot be satisfied by the common child ORDER. All ORDERS have one associated SALES REPRESENTATIVE but not all CUSTOMERs have placed an ORDER. If the common child (ORDER) was used to replace the many-to-many relation, CUSTOMERs without an ORDER would not be able to have an assigned SALES REPRESENTATIVE. Once an Order is placed, the common child is valid. Because the user needs to associate SALES REPRESENTATIVEs with CUSTOMERs even when an order has not been placed, the common child is not a valid replacement for all occurrences of the many-to-many relation.

Return/Credit is also a common child for CUSTOMER and SALES REPRESENTATIVE. It cannot be used because few CUSTOMERs have associated RETURN/CREDITS. To resolve the many-to-many relation a pseudo-child is created.

Figures 5-10(a) and 5-10(b) illustrate the modified relation report and modified linkage diagram after resolving the many-to-many relations of Fig. 5-5.

Network DBMS. Most network data base management systems implement many-to-many relations by redundantly storing the data. The method of creating a pseudo-child usually does not improve a network DBMS's efficiency. Therefore, a many-to-many relation which can-

---

Relation:	BILL OF LADING to CARRIER
Relation Type:	Many-to-many
Description:	A pseudo-child is created called BILL OF LADING to CAR-RIER.

Relation:	GEOGRAPHIC LOCATION to SALES REPRESENTATIVE
Relation Type:	Many-to-many
Description:	Common parent using the entity REGION

Relation:	SALES REPRESENTATIVE to CUSTOMER
Relation Type:	Many-to-many
Description:	A pseudo-child is created called SALES REPRESENTATIVE to CUSTOMER.

Fig. 5-10(a). Modified relations report: many-to-many relations (hierarchical).

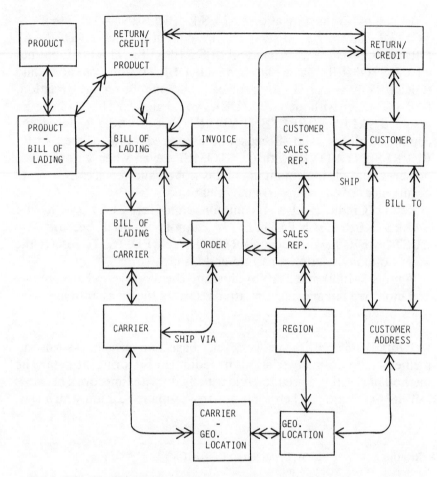

Fig. 5-10(b). Modified linkage diagram: many-to-many relations (hierarchical).

not be resolved by a common child or common parent is left in the structural data model's linkage diagram. The change to the linkage diagram for a network DBMS is the elimination of the relation GEO-GRAPHIC LOCATION to SALES REPRESENTATIVE because it is replaced by a common parent. Since pseudo-child entities are not created for network DBMSs, the relations BILL OF LADING to CARRIER and SALES REPRESENTATIVE to CUSTOMER remain in the diagram. The modified relation report and modified linkage diagram for network DBMSs is shown in Figs. 5–11(a) and 5–11(b).

The hierarchical modified linkage diagram (Fig. 5–10) will be used to show steps 3–6. Step 7 will show the resulting logical data structures for both hierarchical and network data base management systems.

Modify Identity Relations (Step 3)

An identity is a relation between two entities which is a one-to-one relation. Identities are modified in the structural data model's linkage diagram to draw valid logical data structures. The logical data structure implies a parent–child relation while the identity implies an equal or parent-to-parent relation. The choice of one entity subordinate to the other is not to be made at this point. It is resolved during physical data base design, based on information provided in the usage model.

For each identity modify the linkage diagram as follows:

1. For each entity involved in the identity, place 'I = X' below the entity's name, where X is the name of the other entity.
2. Eliminate the one-to-one (identity) relation between the two entities.

The INVOICE and BILL OF LADING entities in Fig. 5–5 have an identity relation between them. The relation is removed from the

Relation:	BILL OF LADING to CARRIER
Relation Type:	Many-to-many
Description:	Not changed because a common parent and common child were not found
Relation:	GEOGRAPHIC LOCATION to SALES REPRESENTATIVE
Relation Type:	Many-to-many
Description:	Common parent using the entity REGION.
Relation:	SALES REPRESENTATIVE to CUSTOMER
Relation Type:	Many-to-many
Description:	Not changed because a common parent and a common child were not found

Fig. 5–11(a). Modified linkage diagram: modified relations report (network).

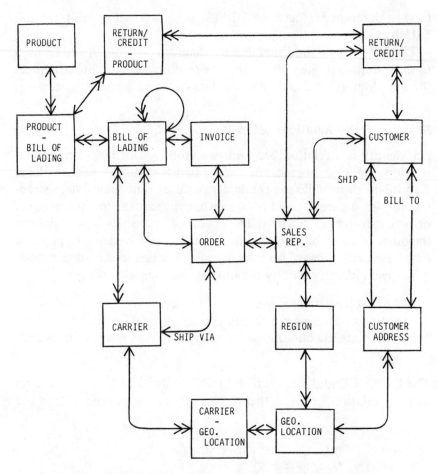

Fig. 5-11(b). Modified linkage diagram: many-to-many relations (network).

linkage diagram, its existence is marked in the entity boxes, and it is documented in the modified relations report, as shown in Figs. 5-12(a) and 5-12(b).

Identify Potentially Redundant Entities (Step 4)

An entity which has more than one complex relation (the many end of the relation) entering it is potentially redundant. The redundancy is caused by its being subordinate to multiple entities and the fact that it

Relation: INVOICE to BILL OF LADING
Relation Type: Identity
Description: The INVOICE and BILL OF LADING entities are marked as
                identities

Fig. 5-12(a). Modified relations report: identity relations.

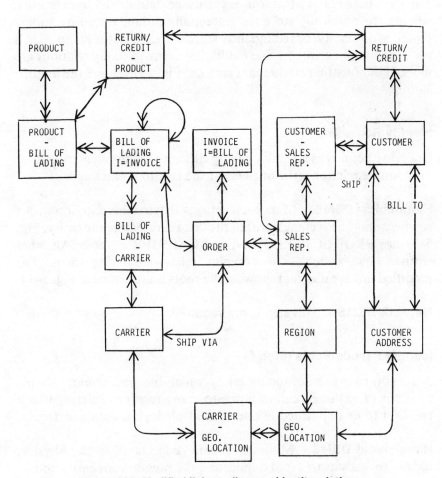

Fig. 5-12(b). Modified linkage diagram: identity relations.

can exist in two or more logical data structures. In Figs. 5–12(a) and 5–12(b), the entities BILL OF LADING, PRODUCT–BILL OF LADING, RETURN/CREDIT, CUSTOMER, ORDER, SALES REPRESENTATIVE–CUSTOMER, RETURN/CREDIT–PRODUCT and CARRIER–GEOGRAPHIC LOCATION have two or more complex relations entering them and are considered potentially redundant entities. These entities could be subordinate (child) to two or more entities. Mark these entities on the modified linkage diagram by drawing a line across the top of the entity box to remind you that a design decision must be made when developing the physical data base. The data base administrator uses the usage data model to determine whether to physically store the potentially redundant entity subordinate to one entity, or redundantly store it under multiple entities. All pseudo-children created while modifying many-to-many relations are marked as potentially redundant entities. Fig. 5–13 shows the modifications.

Identify Roots (Step 5)

Roots are defined as an entity having either no relations entering it, or only simple relations (the one end of the relation) entering it.

Hierarchical DBMS. Mark each entity satisfying this criterion with a smaller solid-line rectangle within the box representing the entity. Fig. 5–13 has PRODUCT, REGION, and CARRIER·as roots. All other entities have at least one complex relation entering them. The modified linkage diagram showing the roots is illustrated in Fig. 5–14.

Network DBMS. This step is not required.

Identify Pseudo-Roots (Step 6)

A pseudo-root is a redundant entity which has one or more simple relations (The "one" end of a one-to-many relation) entering which causes it to be duplicated in one or multiple logical data structures.

Hierarchical DBMS. Minimizing data redundancy in the physical data base leads us to avoid duplicating the pseudo-root entity and its

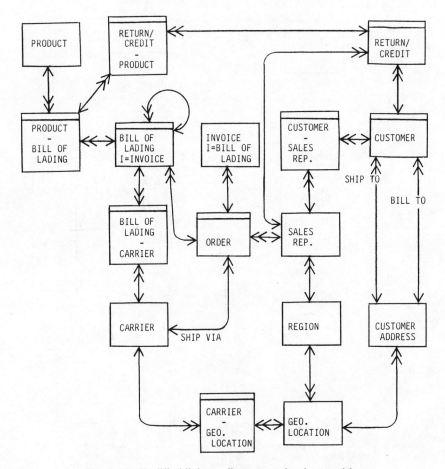

Fig. 5-13. Modified linkage diagram: redundant entities.

children. At this time in data base design, these entities are high-lighted. During physical data base design, the data base administrator uses the usage date model to determine physical placement of the pseudo-root with its subordinate entities (children) and the degree of data redundancy.

All pseudo-root entities are marked with a smaller dotted-line box within the box representing the entity. ORDER, CUSTOMER, RE-TURN/CREDIT, and PRODUCT–BILL OF LADING are pseudo-roots in Fig. 5-14. The potentially redundant entities, BILL OF

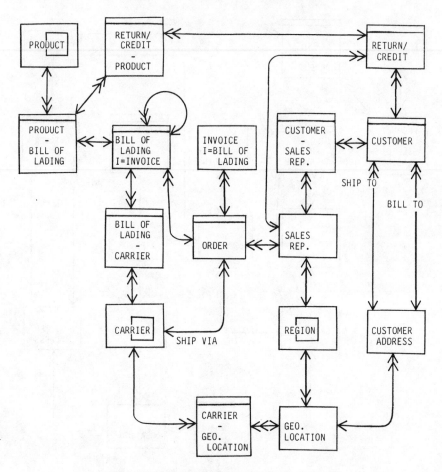

Fig. 5-14. Modified linkage diagram: roots.

LADING, CARRIER–GEOGRAPHIC LOCATION, SALES REP-
RESENTATIVE–CUSTOMER and RETURN/CREDIT–PROD-
UCT are not pseudo-roots because they do not have simple relations
entering them. Fig. 5–15 shows the pseudo-roots marked on the
modified linkage diagram.

Network DBMS. This step is not required.

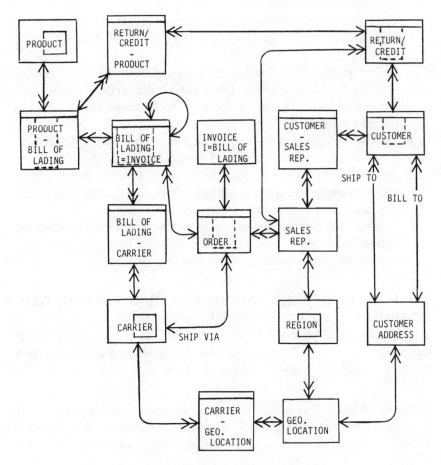

Fig. 5-15. Modified linkage diagram: pseudo-roots.

Develop the Logical Data Structures (Step 7)

Two approaches to developing logical data structures are defined because of differing physical data base implementation techniques required by hierarchical and network data base management systems.

Hierarchical DBMS. Using the modified linkage diagram (Fig. 5-15) and the following rules, a hierarchical DBMS's logical data structures are developed.

1. Choose a root or pseudo-root entity to create the first level of the logical data structure. Draw a box and label it with the entity name.
2. Follow each simple relation entering the root or pseudo-root to identify the child entities. Draw the entities related to the root level of the structure as its children to create the second level of the structure.
3. Follow the simple relations entering each child to create the next level. Draw the entities related to these as their children. Continue the process for as many levels required. The process stops when an entity has either no simple relations entering it, or an entity is marked as a redundant entity.
4. Symbols for redundant entities, pseudo-roots, and identities are shown in the logical data structures.
5. Repeat the process for all roots and pseudo-roots.

In Fig. 5-15, BILL OF LADING–CARRIER, CARRIER–GEO-GRAPHIC LOCATION, and ORDER are potentially redundant and are not examined past the second level. REGION has a four-level logical data structure. The complete set of logical data structures for a hierarchical DBMS is shown in Fig. 5-16.

Network DBMS. The modified linkage diagram developed in steps 1 through 4 is the network DBMS's logical data structure. The network DBMS's logical data structure for the example is shown in Fig. 5-17.

Special Situations: Entity Related to Itself

This special situation requires special handling in the development of logical data structures. For a one-to-many relation, as in the MAN-AGER to EMPLOYEE relation shown in Chapter 3, Fig. 3-18 and 3-19, the logical data structure is drawn as shown in Fig. 5-18. Both the parent and child entities are the EMPLOYEE entity; however, the child entity is qualified by the relation's name, MANAGER. The entity–data item list for the EMPLOYEE (MANAGER) entity contains the primary key data items Employee Number and Manager Employee Number. This indicates that the second primary key data item

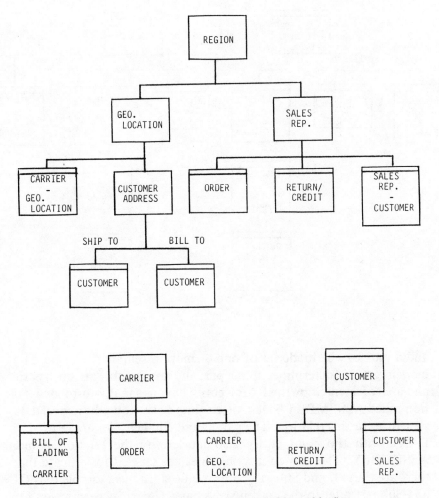

Fig. 5-16. Logical data structures (hierarchical).

is the Employee Number of the Manager. In the data dictionary, a synonym for Employee Number is entered called Manager Employee Number, as shown in Fig. 5–18.

A many-to-many relation for an entity related to itself is drawn the same way as a one-to-many relation, except that two lines are drawn to connect the parent and child entities. For example, an assembly of products in a production environment is made up of one or more parts

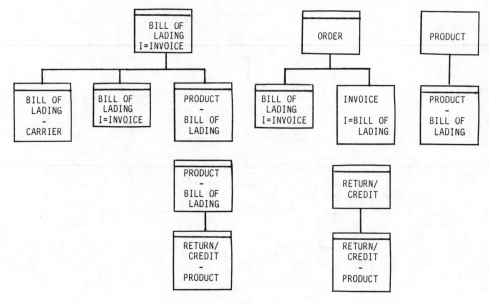

Fig. 5-16. (Cont.)

and a part can be made up of one or more assemblies. During data modeling it was determined that a part and an assembly are both parts and are represented by the PART entity having a many-to-many relation called ASSEMBLY back to itself. Fig. 5-19 shows the logical data structure for this relation. The parent and child entities are labeled as PART with the child entity also labeled by the relation name, ASSEMBLY. The two connecting lines are labeled to indicate that there are Part Of and Subpart paths required. In this example Part Of and Subpart refer to the makeup of a part. The entity description for PART is modified to indicate this information. A new entity ASSEMBLY PART is defined and its entity–data item list contains the primary key of Part Number and Assembly Part Number. Assembly Part Number is defined as a synonym for Part Number.

DEVELOPMENT OF THE RELATIONAL STRUCTURAL DATA MODEL

Even though the normalized data model should translate directly into a relational DBMS, it does not. The relations connecting the entities

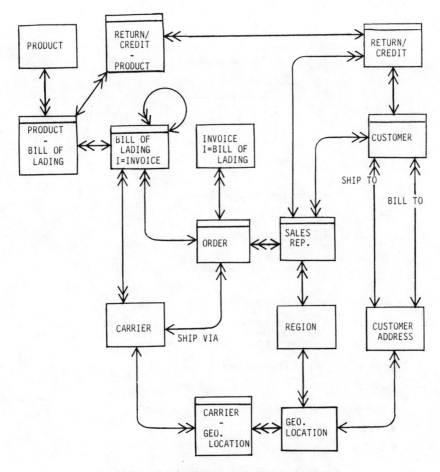

Fig. 5-17. Logical data structures (network).

must be evaluated and the entities modified to enable the joining of tables. To perform relational operations on a set of normalized entities, a relational DBMS requires the entities to contain common or redundant data items. Establishing redundant data items is done by resolving the following three types of relation:

1. Identity relations
2. One-to-many relations
3. Many-to-many relations

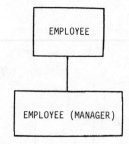

Entity Name: EMPLOYEE (MANAGER)

Description: Identifies the Employees who work for a Manager and
                the Manager of an Employee..

Entity Type: Normalized

Business Functions Supported: Personnel, Payroll

Composed Of: Employee Number
                Manager Employee Number

Data Item Name: Employee Number

Description: A unique code identifying an Employee of the company, a
             retired employee or a person who was hired as a full time
             employee but has since left the company.

Synonym: Manager Employee Number.

Derivation: Not Applicable.

Standard-Value-Set: 10 characters

Format: NNNNNNNNNA

Composed Of: Not Applicable

Fig. 5–18. Entity related to itself: one-to-many.

A complete structural data model for a relational DBMS is shown in
Appendix A.

Resolve Identity Relations

An identity (one-to-one) relation is removed by taking the primary key
data item(s) from each entity and placing them in the other's entity–data item list. Using Fig. 5–3, there is one identity relation, IN-
VOICE to BILL OF LADING. The modification adds the primary

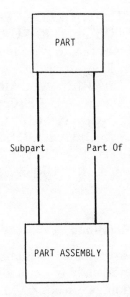

Fig. 5-19. Entity related to itself: many-to-many.

key of INVOICE, Invoice Number, to BILL OF LADING's entity-data item list and Bill of Lading Number from BILL OF
LADING to the entity-data item list of INVOICE.

Resolve One-to-Many Relations

The primary key of the entity at the one (single arrowhead) end of the
relation is placed in the entity-data item list of the entity at the many
(double arrowhead) end of the relation. This is done when the primary
key data items are not already contained in the "many" entity's en-
tity-data item list. In Fig. 5-3, the following one-to-many relations re-
quire the addition of the primary key data item in the many entity:
BILL OF LADING to BILL OF LADING, BILL OF LADING to
ORDER, BILL OF LADING to RETURN/CREDIT-PRODUCT,
CARRIER to ORDER, CUSTOMER Ship to CUSTOMER AD-
DRESS, CUSTOMER Bill to CUSTOMER ADDRESS, INVOICE to
ORDER, GEOGRAPHIC LOCATION to REGION, ORDER to
REGION, ORDER to SALES REPRESENTATIVE, BILL OF LAD-

ING-PRODUCT to RETURN/CREDIT-PRODUCT, REGION to SALES REPRESENTATIVE, and RETURN/CREDIT to SALES REPRESENTATIVE. Eight relations do not require the changes to the entity-data item lists. They are: BILL OF LADING to BILL OF LADING-PRODUCT, CARRIER to CARRIER-GEOGRAPHIC LOCATION, CARRIER-GEOGRAPHIC LOCATION to GEO-GRAPHIC LOCATION, CUSTOMER to RETURN/CREDIT, CUSTOMER ADDRESS to GEOGRAPHIC LOCATION, PROD-UCT to BILL OF LADING-PRODUCT, PRODUCT to RETURN/CREDIT-PRODUCT, and RETURN/CREDIT to RETURN/CREDIT-PRODUCT.

Resolve Many-to-Many Relations

Many-to-many relations are handled the same as for hierarchical/network DBMSs. If a common child or common parent cannot resolve the many-to-many relation, a pseudo-child entity is created. This pseudo-child becomes a table containing only the primary keys of the two entities that form the many-to-many relations. These data items become the primary key of the pseudo-child. The many-to-many relation GEOGRAPHIC LOCATION to SALES REPRESENTATIVE in Fig. 5-3 is satisfied by the common parent REGION. BILL OF LADING to CARRIER and CUSTOMER to SALES REPRESEN-TATIVE require the creation of pseudo-child entities. The entity-data item lists of the pseudo-children contain the primary keys of the entities. For BILL OF LADING to CARRIER it contains Bill of Lading Number and Carrier Number. For CUSTOMER to SALES REPRESENTATIVE it contains Sales Representative Number and Customer Number.

Relational Logical Data Structure

A revised entity-data item list and logical data structure (see Appendix A) are created to document the Relational DBMS's structural data model. The logical data structure is the normalized data model's linkage diagram with the relations resolved. The revised entity-data item list reflects the addition of the data items used to relate entities and the creation of pseudo-child entities.

REVIEW THE LOGICAL DATA STRUCTURES

After completing the logical data structures, they must be evaluated for:

- Reasonableness: Do they represent the relations between entities in a rational, practical structure?
- Completeness: Do they represent all the relations between entities based on current knowledge of the system or systems that will use them?

The material required for the review includes the normalized data model, the usage data model, the logical data structure, and the modified relation reports.

The logical data structure represents known relations between entities which if implemented as is, satisfy current and many future uses of the data. However, systems using the structure may not require all the entities or relations. To determine which are needed, the usage data model is used. The logical data structure can satisfy the user's requirements for data since it directly implements the user environment's entities and relations. Any decisions not to implement the entities and relations or to implement them in a different structural format must be made carefully and based on access information from the usage data model. Deviations are caused by the need to satisfy system performance or data security requirements. To identify performance or security problems, systems are designed assuming the structural data model's logical data structure. Only then can potential problems be identified. Identification and resolution are made prior to beginning program design, with the reasons for the performance deviations documented with the logical data structures.

The logical data structures also represent the user environment in a format that can be implemented in a nonrelational DBMS. It is important to note that the logical data structure does not imply the direction in which the relations are used or should be used. What it does show is that a relation exists. Hierarchical data base management systems like IMS and System 2000 work most efficiently when data are accessed in a one-to-many (top-to-bottom) direction. The logical data structures identify the most efficient one-to-many hierarchies for their use.

Implementing the logical data structure in a relational DBMS is straightforward: the entities become the relational DBMS's tables. The purpose of the usage data model is to establish the number of rows or records per table based on the volume estimates, and the index data or entry points using the access requirements. If the DBMS allows predefined joins, the usage data model will identify these. This will allow faster processing.

CONCLUSION

When you compare the logical data structures created in this chapter with the Documentation Example of Appendix A, they are not the same. This is because a subset of the data environment was used. If the normalized data model is developed for the entire company, the resulting logical data structures would satisfy all systems and only change when the company changes the way it does business. Developing the normalized data model for a system will result in changes to the logical data structure as the normalized data model and logical data structure are expanded to include other systems. To avoid costly changes to existing data bases there are two choices: either duplicate the data in another data base or expand the scope of analysis for normalization. Duplicating data causes many problems previously mentioned. Expanding the scope of analysis is the recommended approach and is discussed in the data planning chapter.

6. PHYSICAL DATA BASE DESIGN OVERVIEW

INTRODUCTION

Physical data base design requires the normalized, usage, and structural data models and technical knowledge of the chosen data base management system (DBMS). In physical data base design the normalized entities become segments or repeating groups and the relations become the hierarchical or network mappings with the ideal physical implementation shown by the Structural Data Model. For relational Data Base Management Systems, the entities and relations become tables. In all DBMSs, security and performance considerations need to be resolved.

This book does not define the work activities to develop the physical design for a specific Data Base Management System. It does present the physical data base structures without the tuning and accessing considerations having been resolved. Resolving these concerns utilizes the physical data base structures and technical information on the DBMS which is available from the DBMS vendor.

The three data models shorten the physical data base design time and provide for a physical data base completed prior to program design. These techniques have been used to design many data bases quickly and efficiently. A data base administrator (DBA) knowledgeable in the technical aspects of the DBMS is a must to design and implement the physical data bases.

IMS/VS/DB

Figure 6–1 shows the IMS physical data base structure for the Data Models of Appendix A. It took the IMS Data Base Administrator about 2 weeks to establish the physical design of four multiple seg-

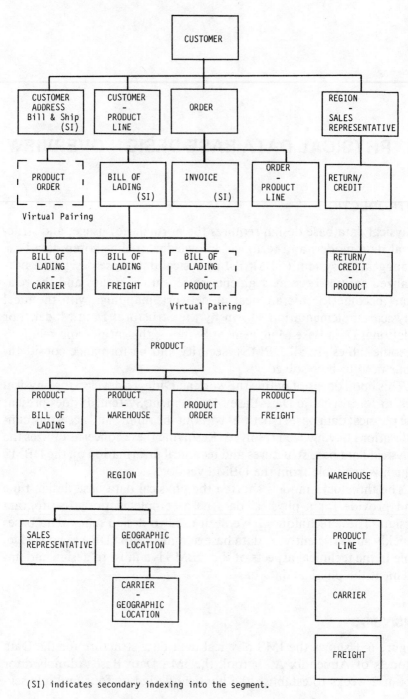

(SI) indicates secondary indexing into the segment.

Fig. 6-1. IMS physical data base structures.

ment data bases and four single segment data bases (tables). In IMS each entity becomes a segment.

To provide access and improve performance, the following changes were made to the normalized entities. In the CUSTOMER data base, the CUSTOMER ADDRESS segment had the following data items added to it: a flag to indicate Ship To, Bill to, or both; Zip Code the primary key of GEOGRAPHIC LOCATION; and Region Code the primary key of REGION. The ORDER segment has two data items—Carrier Number the primary key of CARRIER and Sales Representative Name the primary key of SALES REPRESENTATIVE—added to it to provide an access path from the ORDER segment to those segments. In addition, a new segment, REGION—SALES REPRESENTATIVE, is created as a child of CUSTOMER and parent of REGION/CREDIT with its data items being the primary keys of the segments REGION (Region Code) and SALES REPRE-SENTATIVE (Sales Representative Name). This is done to provide access to those segments through the CUSTOMER segment. The BILL OF LADING segment has the data item Freight Code added to it. To handle potentially redundant entities, the CUSTOMER data base has a virtual paired segment, PRODUCT ORDER, which provides access to its physically paired segments in the PRODUCT data base. Another virtual paired segment PRODUCT–BILL OF LAD-ING in this data base has its physically paired segment in the PROD-UCT data base. The PRODUCT data base has the data item Product Line Code added to the PRODUCT segment which handles access to the PRODUCT LINE segment through the PRODUCT segment. BILL OF LADING–PRODUCT and PRODUCT ORDER are the physical segments of the virtual paired segments contained in the CUSTOMER data base.

Secondary indexes have been established in the BILL OF LADING, INVOICE, and CUSTOMER ADDRESS segments to provide direct access to those segments as required by the usage data model. BILL OF LADING's secondary index is Bill of Lading Number, and In-voice Number is the secondary index for the INVOICE segment. Three secondary indexes are established in CUSTOMER ADDRESS to satisfy access via the Region Code and Zip Code data items. Both secondary index data items have a target of the CUSTOMER seg-ment.

SYSTEM 2000

The translation of the Structural Data Model of Appendix A into a System 2000 physical data base structure was completed by the System 2000 data base designer in one week. The first step is to establish an initial physical design using only the structural data model. Then the physical data base structures are built using the usage data model and the designer's knowledge of System 2000.

Initial Physical Design

Since System 2000 can handle a many-to-many relation, any pseudo-entities created during the structural data model are removed and replaced by the many-to-many relation. In Appendix A's structural data model, three pseudo-entities were created: BILL OF LADING–CARRIER, CUSTOMER–PRODUCT LINE, and SALES REPRESENTATIVE–GEOGRAPHIC LOCATION. Each logical data structure containing any of these pseudo-entities is changed by removing the pseudo-entity and replacing it with the entity at the other end of the original many-to-many relation. For example, in the BILL OF LADING logical data structure, the pseudo-entity BILL OF LADING–CARRIER is removed and replaced by the entity CARRIER. In the CARRIER logical data structure, the entity BILL OF LADING replaces the pseudo-entity BILL OF LADING–CARRIER.

The next step in developing the initial physical design is to change the logical data structures containing a pseudo-root entity as a child entity. Each logical data structure of a root or pseudo-root entity is changed if it contains a pseudo-root entity. This change replaces each pseudo-root, which is a child of another entity, with the pseudo-root's logical data structure. For example, the CARRIER logical data structure contains the pseudo-root entity ORDER. CARRIER's logical data structure is expanded to include the four entities which are children of ORDER (see Fig. 6–2). When this is completed the separate pseudo-root's logical data structure is removed. Fig. 6–2 shows the initial System 2000 physical design for the example in Appendix A.

Physical Data Base Structure

In System 2000 physical data base design, each normalized entity becomes a repeating group. Developing the physical data base struc-

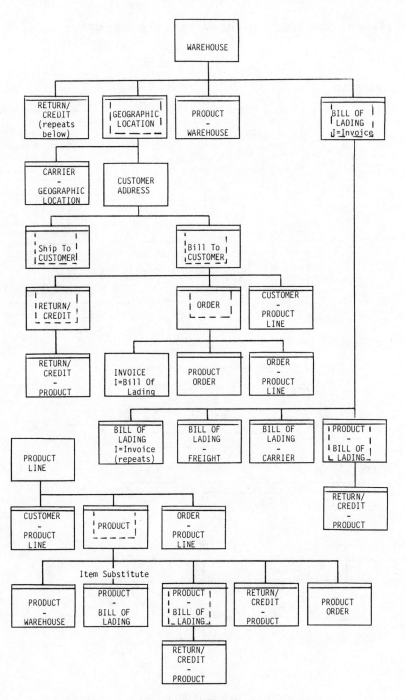

Fig. 6-2. Initial System 2000 physical structures.

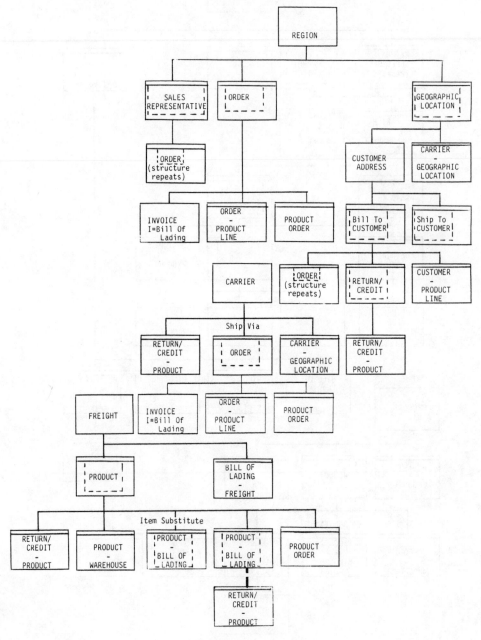

Fig. 6-2. *(Cont.)*

ture (see Fig. 6–3) requires the Usage Data Model a physical data base designer with detailed knowledge of System 2000. The physical data base structure required changes to the three normalized entities: CUSTOMER, ORDER–PRODUCT LINE, and PRODUCT–WAREHOUSE. Two CUSTOMER repeating groups (entities) were established. One as a Ship to CUSTOMER which contains all data items specified in the entity CUSTOMER, and a Bill to CUSTOMER repeating group which only contains the primary key data item (Customer Number). This was done to minimize data redundancy. The repeating groups, ORDER–PRODUCT LINE and PRODUCT–WAREHOUSE, have concatenated keys consisting of their primary key data items to allow direct access to the repeating group via the concatenated key. Additional direct access to the repeating groups (entities) will be established utilizing key fields defined to the data base as systems are defined to use this physical data base.

IDMS

IDMS's physical data base structure was designed in less than one week using the three Data Models of Appendix A. The design shown in Fig. 6–6 uses IDMS's physical design format with the Bachmann symbol used for IDMS designs and the associated abbreviations defined in Fig. 6–4. The entity names, set names, and region/area names used in the diagram use an abbreviation synonym to reduce the names to the space limitations of the Bachmann symbol. Each Bachmann symbol represents one entity and is identified by a 4-digit number and the entity name in the abbreviated form. The relations are represented by a line with the relation given a name and other physical design parameters specified by the physical data base designer. Fig. 6–5 lists the IDMS record and set names as matched to the corresponding names in the data models.

If a many-to-many relation exists in the structural data model, it must be removed by establishing a pseudo-child entity consisting of the primary keys from the two entities connected by the relation as done for the hierarchical DBMS in the Structural Data Model of Chapter 5. Each entity in the structural data model becomes an IDMS "record" and each relation becomes an IDMS "set." For each set, the "one" (single arrowhead) end of the normalized data model's

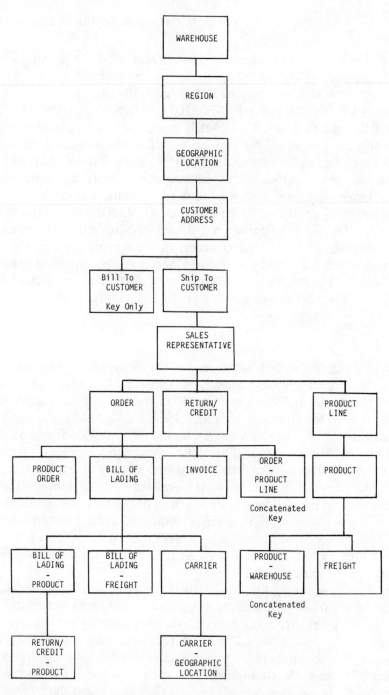

Fig. 6-3. System 2000 physical data base structures.

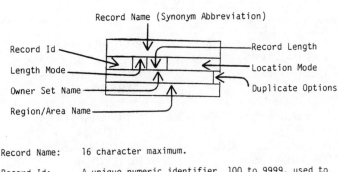

Record Name: 16 character maximum.

Record Id: A unique numeric identifier, 100 to 9999, used to
                identify an IDMS record.

Location Mode:

    CALC   Randomized storage of record occurrences.
    VIA   Record occurrences stored in close proximity of the
                specified owner set.

Record Length: Number of bytes in the record.

Length Mode:

    F   Fixed length records.
    FC   Fixed length and compressed records.
    V   Variable length records (not used if the data has been
                normalized.
    VC   Variable length and compressed records (not used if the
                data has been normalized.

Duplicate Options:

    D   Duplicate record occurrences allowed (never occurrs if
                data is normalized).
    DF   Duplicate CALC records stored first (never occurrs if
                data is normalized).
    DL   Duplicate CALC records stored last (never occurrs if
                data is normalized).
    DN   No duplicate record occurrences allowed.

Region/Area Name: Area containing all occurrences of record type.

Fig. 6-4. IDMS symbol and abbreviation definitions.

relation connecting two entities is defined as the owner member of the
set. The "many" (double arrowhead) end becomes the member of the
set. In the IDMS physical design shown in Fig. 6-6, the member is
identified by a single arrow on the line representing the set. The owner
has no arrowhead pointing to it.

For each set, the designer determines if the relationship between the
owner and member are manditory or optional. This is represented in

NORMALIZED DATA MODEL NAME	IDMS RECORD/SET NAME
BILL OF LADING	BILL OF LADING
BILL OF LADING–FREIGHT	FREIGHT-BILL LAD
BILL OF LADING–PRODUCT	PROD-BILL OF LAD
CARRIER	CARRIER
CARRIER–BILL OF LADING	CARRIER-BILL OF LAD
CARRIER–GEOGRAPHIC LOCATION	CARR-GEO LOC
CUSTOMER	CUSTOMER
CUSTOMER–PRODUCT LINE	PROD LN CUST
CUSTOMER ADDRESS	CUST ADDR
FREIGHT	FREIGHT
GEOGRAPHIC LOCATION	GEO LOC
INVOICE	INVOICE
ORDER	ORDER
ORDER–PRODUCT LINE	ORDER-PROD LN
PRODUCT	PRODUCT
PRODUCT–WAREHOUSE	PROD-WAREHOUSE
PRODUCT LINE	PRODUCT LINE
PRODUCT ORDER	ORDER-PROD
REGION	REGION
RETURN/CREDIT	RETURN CREDIT
RETURN/CREDIT–PRODUCT	RETURN CD PROD
SALES REPRESENTATIVE	SALES REP
WAREHOUSE	WAREHOUSE

NORMALIZED DATA MODEL NAME	IDMS SET NAME ABBREVIATIONS
Address	ADDR
Bill of Lading	BL
Bill to Address	BILL-ADDR
Carrier	CARR
Customer	CUST
Customer Address	CUSTADD
Geographic Location	GL
Invoice	INV
Product	PROD
Product Line	PL
Region	RGN
Return/Credit	RC
Sales Representative	SR
Ship to Address	SHIP-ADDR
Warehouse	WH

Fig. 6-5. IDMS data model names.

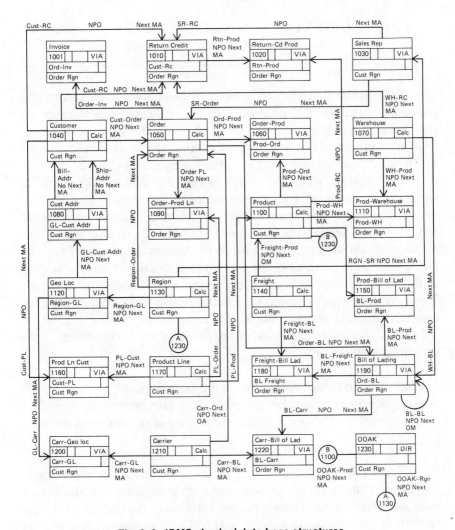

Fig. 6-6. IDMS physical data base structures.

Fig. 6-6 by the following notation on the line representing the set connecting the two records:

'set name' NPO NEXT MA   Next, Prior, and Owner Pointers are mandatory and automatic. These relationships are connect options.

'set name' NPO NEXT OM   Next, Prior, and Owner Pointers are optional and mandatory. These relationships are disconnect options.

"Next" indicates that pointers are established between one record and the next occurrence of the record. "Prior" indicates that pointers are established between one record and the previous occurrence. "Owner" indicates that pointers are established to the Owner record of the set. "Mandatory" indicates the member records related to an owner are deleted when the owner is deleted. When "Optional" is specified, the member records are disconnected from the owner but not deleted when the owner is deleted. "Manual" causes the member records to be added to the data base but not added to a set until commanded to do so by a program. With "automatic" specified, the DBMS software establishes the pointers automatically and must exist at the time the member record occurrences are created or updated. This establishes the required data dependencies that exist in the end-user environment as specified by the usage data model.

For each record, the designer specifies how it is to be stored. Two options are available:

CALC   Randomized storage of record occurrences.

VIA   Record occurrences stored in close proximity to the specified owner. The set in which the record is to be stored must be specified.

Each record has a fixed length because the normalized entity it represents cannot have repeated data items because normalization does not allow them. Therefore, the variable option is not used with records based on third normal form. The last option specifies if duplicate record occurrences can exist. With records based on a normalized data model, duplicate record occurrences are not allowed. Normalization removes this possibility.

Two IDMS "regions" were established based on the usage data model's access statements and volume estimates. They are the Order Region and the Customer Region, abbreviated ORDER RGN and CUST RGN, respectively. The ORDER RGN contains records which are frequently added to, modified, or deleted from the data base. Infrequent updates, additions, or deletions are made to the CUST RGN. This separation aids in tuning the physical data base and data base access.

The OOAK record indicated in Fig. 6–6 is created for the CUST RGN to provide a method to obtain all occurrences of a record type. In this design, it provides access to the REGION and PRODUCT records.

CONDOR

The CONDOR data base structure for Appendix A's Data Models is a set of tables as defined in Appendix A's Structural Data Model for a relational Data Base Management System (see Fig. 6–7). The pictorial

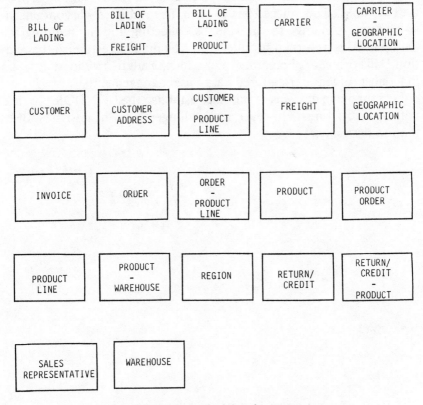

Fig. 6-7. CONDOR physical data base structures.

representation is each entity as a separate table containing the data items specified in the structural data model entity–data item list for a relational data base management system given in Appendix A. The relations are not shown since there are no predefined joins. However, the user should be aware of the valid joins shown in the normalized data model's linkage diagram. It is too easy to create invalid joins simply because two tables contain one or more of the same data items.

For example, a join between PRODUCT–WAREHOUSE and RE-TURN/CREDIT–PRODUCT is possible based on the common data item Product Number. This join, to relate a returned product to the warehouse to which the product was returned, is not valid. The normalized data model did not contain this relation, therefore the system which collects and maintains the data did not establish the data items (foreign keys or relators) required to establish a valid relation between the two tables. The join can be done but the resulting table contains invalid data. A change to the systems collecting and maintaining the data related to returned products must be made to establish the relation. This problem of creating joins which result in invalid tables is an inherent problem in relational data base management systems.

Less than one day was required to establish the CONDOR physical data base structures. However, it took longer to define it to the DBMS than to design it.

7. DATA/DATA BASE ADMINISTRATION

INTRODUCTION

Data/data base administration is responsible for managing and controlling the company's data environment and for coordinating all data information requests. It includes responsibilities for the definition, structuring, security, and efficiency of data and data base(s); and for defining the rules by which data are to be accessed, stored, and protected.

As the manager of the company's data resource, data/data base administration (D/DBA) is responsible to company management for correct and efficient access to the data resource. Plans for new data processing technologies and for the implementation of new systems must involve D/DBA. In addition, D/DBA must be aware of management policies and plans affecting the data resource and ensure that data base plans and policies are consistent with them. The two major functions of data/data base administration are:

- Identification and administration of what should be in the company's data bases, including the definition, modeling, and structuring of data. This is the responsibility of the data administration group.
- Design, implementation, and maintenance of the company's data bases. The data base administration group is responsible for this function.

The basic difference between these two functional responsibilities are the skills required and the user communities served. Data administration requires analysis skills, knowledge of the end-user environment, data planning skills, data modeling skills, and the ability to deal with end-users. Data base administration determines how to implement the data on a computer and requires skills and knowledge of the DBMS being used, and requires the ability to deal with system development personnel and the more technical end-users who use the more advanced software tools.

DATA ADMINISTRATION (DA)

Data administration identifies, defines, plans, and manages the company's data environment as well as develops logical data structures which can be implemented in any data base management system. Data administration's duties include:

- Data planning
- Data modeling
- Developing, implementing, and maintaining data security guidelines
- Establishing and monitoring data dictionary standards
- Training users in data planning, data modeling, and data base concepts
- Consulting with system developers on data related system requirements

Data administration is end-user oriented and concerned with establishing an integrated data environment to provide the end-users with the data they want, in the format they want, and in the time frame in which they require it. The relationship between data administration and the end-users must be one of full confidence.

Understanding end-user requirements has both strategic and tactical implications. Data Administration must be aware of the corporate long-range strategic and tactical plans and both long- and short-range end-user requirements for data. The most common example is the development of different systems, by different user groups, which require the same data or a subset of the same data. Data administration's job is to provide for shared use and common access of data for both user groups. While the short-range plans are to build the systems for specific end-user needs, the company's tactical plans are to integrate the development of data bases using the data planning approach. This requires additional front-end development time for each system, but the long-term benefits to the systems and company outweight the short-term gains of quickly satisfying the immediate need. The short-term gains can create long-term data integrity problems which are avoided by establishing shared or common data bases. Data Administration is responsible for ensuring the company's strategic goal of "providing a data base environment that is an effective and efficient tool for *all* users" is achieved.

Data Planning and Data Modeling

Data administration (DA) identifies, defines, and implements data planning and data modeling as defined in Chapters 2–5 to establish the company's logical data structures. Using the data planning approach (see Chapter 2), DA defines the logical data structures which reflect future developments and the requirements of users.

Data Security

Data administration is responsible for establishing data security and data access authority. The owner/custodian for each normalized entity or data item is identified. Based on the owner/custodian's authorization, who has the authority to retrieve, update or delete data is defined by data administration in the data dictionary. Once this has been established, proper controls must be set up by DBA to prevent and record attempted authority violations of the data base. Certain data may be confidential (for example, personnel data, product research data) and as such security procedures are implemented by DBA to provide adequate data access security.

Data Dictionary

Data administration is responsible for creating and maintaining the data dictionary which contains standard information about the company's data resource. DA assures that the data dictionary is accessible to all authorized users and that they have current information appropriate to their needs. Before new data are added to a data base or file, DA determines whether or not there are existing definitions and descriptions in the dictionary that properly describe these data. If not, new data definitions, descriptions, and cross-references are developed and added.

Data administration assists users in their search for data to satisfy their information requirements. The users and data administration use the data dictionary as the initial source for information on data, determining data availability and sourcing the data. If some data items are not in the existing data bases (not in the data dictionary), DA with the assistance of the users identifies, defines, and describes the data and incorporates it into the existing data models and data dictionary. Then data base administration determines how to implement the modified data models given the existing physical data base structures. The decision to modify existing data bases, or to build new data bases with redundancy, is made by data base administration after considering economics and state-of-the-art technology.

An important function of DA is responsibility for documenting standards, procedures, and guidelines in the data dictionary. In addition, DA is responsible for ensuring that data planning and data modeling projects are documented so that proper, efficient, and continuing utilization of the company's data resource can be achieved. The documentation in the data dictionary must be available and on line for use by end-users, system development personnel, data administration, data base administration, and computer operations.

Data administration is responsible for providing and maintaining documentation on:

- Data planning projects
- Data modeling, including the normalized, usage, and structural data models
- The company's data inventory, including:
  1. Edit and validation rules for data
  2. Present form of data in existing systems
  3. Systems (manual and mechanized) using the data
  4. Data bases or files containing the data
  5. Programs using the data
  6. Users authorized to either read, modify, or delete the data
  7. Owner/custodian of data
- Passwords and user data access authority
- Data security levels and requirements of data items and entities

Training

Training of the end-users and MIS personnel in data base concepts, data planning, data modeling, data dictionary, and data security is the responsibility of data administration. The level of detail varies based on the audience and the individual's level of need.

Consulting

DA works with people and the tools which must support what the people are trying to accomplish with the data resources. The data consulting environment includes the integration of data, realignment of traditional user and MIS functions, and establishment of new relationships among the people involved with data and data bases. Resistance to the eventual changes will be evident and must be dealt with individually and objectively. The data administration staff must be able to sell its concepts using diplomacy and yet be firm in their resolve and direction. DA requires the support of MIS and end-users and, in return, must support them by making data available when they need it.

DATA BASE ADMINISTRATION (DBA)

Data Base Administration performs activities and makes the decisions that establish and maintain the company's operational and informational data bases. DBA performs technical design and implementation of data-administration-developed logical data structures in a DBMS which will satisfy the end-users's data requirements. To achieve the end-users' requirements and ensure performance, DBA uses analytical tools (for example, prototyping) to maximize data access and performance. The data base administration group is the company's expert on data base management systems (DBMSs) used in the company. Data base administration is concerned with:

- Designing and implementing physical data bases
- Establishing system data security and access authorization
- Supporting system development personnel
- Documenting physical data base design requirements in the data dictionary

- Determining, monitoring, and tuning data base physical storage requirements
- Establishing, monitoring, and tuning data base access and manipulation
- Establishing and enforcing data base standards and guidelines
- Maintaining data base management system software

The primary interface with the vendors of the company's data base products is the responsibility of DBA. This includes maintaining communications with the vendors to maintain state-of-the-art knowledge of the software and hardware developments and to enhance the data base management system.

Physical Data Base Design

The physical data base structures are designed from the data models with the primary objective of satisfying end-user's requirements for accessing data. Physical data base design requires DBA to have technical expertise in the DBMS software and in translating logical data structures in to the DBMS physical structures. DBA maximizes the flexibility of data access with performance being a tuning concern. With today's CPU processing speeds, performance can often be met with the logical data structures implemented as is.

Efficient physical structuring requires expertise on the part of data base administration in translating DA's logical data structures. First, DBA weighs the advantages of a given set of physical structures against its costs in terms of CPU and DASD space required and in the degradation of data base access performance. The primary concern is data availability. The solution depends on a variety of factors such as: logical data format and relationships, physical data format and relationships, access methods, frequencies of access, physical storage requirements, scheduling and response time considerations, and search strategies. All needs may not be economically met within a single data base using current technology. Redundant data or multiple data bases containing the same data may be required for performance. This use of redundant data is acceptable provided it is planned and the integrity of the data bases can be maintained.

To generate the physical data base, DBA requires or establishes the following and is responsible for and controls the physical data base descriptions:

- Data base name
- Data set types and names
- Security specifications
- Data item names
- Data base record size and description
- Data item size and representation
- Estimated entity frequencies and volumes
- Entity and data relationships
- Space allocations
- Storage device specifications
- Estimated access volumes
- Response time requirements

Security and Access Authorization

Protection of the physical data resource is a primary responsibility of data base administration. The general considerations for data base protection are data base access and manipulation; data base integrity, backup, restart, and recovery; and identification of security and access violations or attempted violations. DBA reviews these items and decides the degree to which they apply to each system and data base. To achieve this, data base administration monitors data access and manipulation of the data base, with access or security violation brought to the attention of the company's security administrator for the appropriate action. This responsibility must be clearly specified in the company's data policy (see Appendix E). DBA monitors data access and manipulation of the data base, and handles attempted security or access violations. Without monitoring data access and manipulation little control or security can be achieved in the data base environment. Lack of control results in serious data integrity and serious data security problems.

To protect the data base and help ensure data integrity the DBA ensures that an audit trail of activity against the data base is established in the system by using the DBMS audit tools. The audit function is used to detect missing data, late transaction reporting, and untimely error correction.

System Development Support

Data base administration works with each system development project to assist in identifying the subschemas required to support the system. DBA defines for system developers the logical view and design of how each program will access the data base. Then the subschema and program access specifications are defined to the DBMS and data dictionary. Systems are limited to access and manipulation of logic or subschema. Only DBA needs to know the physical counts, structure, and relationships of physical data bases. DBA is responsible for developing or acquiring data base utility function to:

- Create and test data bases which represent all aspects of real data bases
- Provide backup and recovery for data bases
- Provide automated reports on data integrity

DBA participates in system and program testing to help ensure that the programs work correctly and do not introduce data integrity problems in the data base. This includes: developing and providing test data base, reviewing and providing program data base access and data base use, and assisting in developing testing procedures.

Data Dictionary

Defining and maintaining information about the physical data bases in the data dictionary is the responsibility of data base administration. Since data administration determined whether the data existed or not, DBA determines whether to duplicate the physical data base or establish a common/shared data base. Whichever is chosen is documented in the data dictionary with the reason why and with its physical data base definition. In addition, DBA is responsible for providing and maintaining adequate documentation in the data dictionary such as:

- The physical data structures
- Physical attributes of data (size, format, etc.)
- Data base and program cross-references
- The physical storage medium, including the location, allocation, and utilization of storage space

- Data base usage
- The relationships between transactions and data bases
- DBMS performance and usage measurements which include resources used and frequency of usage, users serviced, and procedures for monitoring the frequency and performance
- Backup and recovery requirements, including frequency, facilities required, and schedules
- Recovery and restart procedures
- Data base testing facilities, including procedures for creating test data bases, testing criteria, and program acceptance criteria.

Physical Storage

Using the usage data model as a starting point, data base administration determines the type and amount of physical storage required by the data bases. This includes the following information, which affects space allocations:

- Entity (table, segment or repeating group) volumes
- Relations volume
- Anticipated growth
- Addition and deletion of data
- Data representation
- Blocking factor
- Data compression methods

Since tradeoffs between minimizing storage and maximizing data accessibility must be made, data base administration must maximize data accessibility while minimizing physical data base storage.

Data Base Access and Manipulation

Who has the right to access or modify the content of data is implemented by data base administration with the owner/custodian of the data granting the right. Once the authority is established, proper controls must be in place to ensure that attempted security violators do not access the data when they are attempted. They must be stopped and the violator be identified. Limited data access by terminal location, terminal identification, and data encryption can be used to ensure greater data security and integrity. These are in addition to software security controls such as passwords.

Complete audit trails of data base activity are required to restore a data base. To do this, DBA ensures that a copy of the input transaction and its user identification is saved and a copy of the data base prior to each update, addition, or removal are kept on a data base log. If data base problems occur, the copies of the data base accesses and input transactions aid in determining the cause of data integrity problems. These logs enable data base administration to restore the data base to just prior to the transaction causing the error or prior to the transaction being processed at the time the error occurred.

Data Base Standards

DBA is responsible for establishing and ensuring that standards, procedures, and guidelines are established and followed by systems development and computer operations when dealing with data bases. DBA establishes data base related operating procedures, establishes restart and recovery procedures, and establishes special data base utilities. DBA works with computer operations personnel to develop formal and documented procedures for data base related systems on the computer.

Maintaining DBMS Software

DBA is responsible for the continued stable performance of the data base software and hardware configuration. This involves the continued monitoring and tuning of the software configuration (DBMS and operating systems) to support systems and data base. Data base administration reviews all changes provided by software vendors as to their impact on the data base environment. New releases and fixes to the data base management system software are installed, tested, and integrated into the operational DBMS environment by DBA. New data base related software and new data base management systems are reviewed and evaluated as to their applicability to the company's data environment.

DATA/DATA BASE ADMINISTRATION ORGANIZATION

D/DBA works with systems development personnel and end-users prior to and during all phases of system development. D/DBA provides the technical expertise necessary to identify and define data requirements, and for structuring data to support the business as well as the system's processes. Once the data bases are operational, D/DBA continues to: interact with end-users to provide them with access to data, interact with the system development staff to resolve data base operational problems, and to tune the data base to meet data access and performance requirements.

The issue to be addressed is the internal organization of Data/Data Base Administration, as shown in Fig. 7-1. D/DBA is based on centralizing the tasks of data planning and data base design, operation, and control. This centralization can make D/DBA incompatible with a decentralized data processing organization. However, an organization's requirements for coordination of certain centralized tasks can result in the formation of a centralized D/DBA group in decentralized

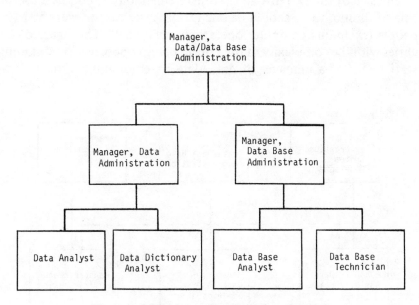

Fig. 7-1. D/DBA internal organization structure.

environments or part of the D/DBA group's tasks can be delegated to a decentralized D/DBA group formed within each decentralized data processing group. If a standards or central DP group exists in a decentralized environment, a D/DBA consultant group is created to manage and establish cooperation and coordination among the several distributed D/DBA groups.

In organizations with decentralized systems development groups, two D/DBA organization structures are possible. First, D/DBA is part of the centralized DP organization acting as a support, consultant, and management role supporting the decentralized systems development groups on an as requested basis. To make this work, D/DBA's management reporting level must equal or exceed that of the decentralized groups they support. Second, the D/DBA staff is divided to support each decentralized system development group on a permanent basis rather than as as needed basis. The DBA staff remains centralized while the data administration staff is decentralized with dotted line reporting to the systems development staff manager/director (see Fig. 7-2).

The size of the D/DBA staff varies tremendously, but, as a useful rule of thumb, there should be one D/DBA person for every 50 MIS people (excluding computer operations personnel). The figure of 50 varies with the complexity of the DBMS being supported. A minimum staff size is 5: a manager of data/data base administration, a data

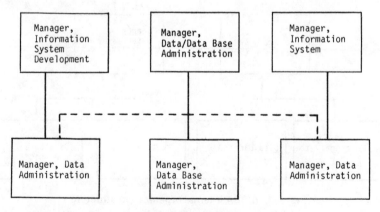

Fig. 7-2. Decentralized D/DBA reporting.

analyst, a data dictionary analyst, a data base analyst, and data base technician. Organizations with a smaller staff size (less than 1 per 50) will have a staff that is not adequate to the task and will fail to achieve an integrated data base environment which manages data as a company resource.

Data Analyst

The data analyst's functions are described in the data planning, normalized data model, usage data model, and structural data model chapters.

Data Dictionary Analyst

The data dictionary analyst performs varied functions on the D/DBA staff. The major function is to manage and control access to the central source of data, the data dictionary. The analyst is responsible for developing, implementing, and maintaining methods, procedures, and standards related to data and data bases. The data dictionary analyst must be an individual with strong communication skills and technical knowledge of how the data dictionary works. Additionally, the analyst must recognize that standards need to reflect the users' input rather than being imposed on users.

Data Base Analyst

Data base analysts require knowledge of the DBMS and how to implement the data models in it. In addition, they require technical skills to specify, tune, and optimize the physical data base. They interact with system development personnel to develop data base views to support program development. Their tasks include:

- Evaluating alternative data base structures and selecting the optimal structure
- Using prototype mechanisms to simulate data base performance and modify data base designs as required
- Providing programmer analysts with the data base definitions and entering those definitions into a data dictionary

- Conducting performance measurements to determine when data base structures require modification
- Monitoring and reorganizing data bases as required

Data Base Technician

The data base technician is the DBMS software technical expert who is responsible for overall DBMS performance and support. While the data base analyst is concerned with data base design and system issues, the data base technician is concerned with data and data base security, data base system performance, data base hardware and software configuration and performance, and the overall data base design and its impact on the data processing center. The data base technician is also responsible for ensuring that the data base(s) can be restored to their proper state in the event of destruction or damage.

Sample position descriptions for the D/DBA organization are contained in Appendix C. They provide a framework for establishing the various D/DBA positions. Since each company will tailor them to meet their own needs, hopefully they will serve to establish some commonality between the positions in the various companies which is lacking today.

8. HOW TO START

INTRODUCTION

Since each company is unique in its implementation and stage of data processing development and level of sophistication, only guidelines on how to start can be given for establishing data planning, data modeling, and data/data base administration. Most of the current approaches to the development of management information systems are directed at designing a system to process a specific set of functions or operations. In this environment:

- Systems are designed in isolation often redundantly collecting data.
- Effective organization and future use of data has been ignored or given cursory attention.
- Data design has proceeded by considering *only* the system's operations on the data.
- Unforeseen and varied requests for data are difficult to handle.
- End-users resort to micros to avoid the MIS organization's inability to satisfy their information requirements.

Even in this environment users expect to easily obtain information from a data base simply because the data has been collected and stored in a data base management system. This is not always so.

To satisfy the growing information needs of the business, data bases must be developed to satisfy the company's information requirements in addition to system needs. Data bases need to be designed based on data relationships as perceived by the end-user community, not based on data usage by any particular system. The methods and procedures to build these flexible data bases are specified in Chapters 1-5.

Establishing data planning, data modeling, and data/data base administration should be implemented and managed as any MIS project.

To begin, the Data/Data Base Administration organization is established, to identify, define, implement, and maintain the company's:

- Data planning efforts
- Common data terminology
- Data modeling approach
- Data inventory
- Logical data structures
- Long-range system plans based on data planning

Numerous problems must be overcome before the data planning project(s) can be successfully begun. Most of the problems are people oriented and are related to people's resistance to change, political sensitivity, job security, and overlapping responsibilities. What is seen is the symptoms of these problems, which are: procrastination, passive resistance, general unresponsiveness, appeals to management, trivial disagreements, argumentativeness, and unavailability. These must be dealt with by anticipating them and avoiding them through active selling, education, training, and communications. Selling the concepts, approach, and benefits increases the chances for success. However, different selling approaches are required to sell the three audiences: company management, end-users, and MIS personnel. To sell each audience requires objectives and strategies to be developed and tailored to their specific needs and concerns.

Selling Company Management

To sell company management, the primary objective is to have them realize and accept that managing the company's data resource is as essential to the management of the company as the management any other company resource. Company management must realize the problems in obtaining the information required to run the business and the amount of work their staff goes through to obtain the information they require to manage the business.

In one company, a member of the company's top management

agreed to commit people and money to start a data planning project because he accepted the concept and believed that it was necessary for his organization to remain competitive into the future. He realized that he does get the information required to make decisions, but he understands the problems his staff has in obtaining the information. What occurred during the year before his commitment was MIS trying to sell the concept to company management, end-user management, and its own personnel. In selling company management one should stress the following approaches:

- Communication between company management and MIS should be improved by establishing a common understanding of business strategic plans so that MIS and company management can develop and implement tactical system plans and data plans.
- Management should be made aware of what is happening in MIS, where the company is headed with MIS, and how MIS fits in with the company's strategic and tactical plans.

In addition to selling data/data base administration to company management, tangible and intangible benefits are also required. Some success has been achieved using the traditional benefits of data base such as:

- *More data sharing* because the data structures are based upon the organization's definition of data, not a specific system's
- *More consistent information* because of standard terminology and definitions
- *Increased knowledge of data availability* because of a centralized, mechanized inventory of information about data
- *Better systems planning* as the approach fosters the integration of systems' functions based upon the commonality of data
- *Reduces costs* by minimizing data analysis efforts, by providing initial physical structures much earlier in the development cycle, and by reducing maintenance efforts with more common input/ update processing

However, to succeed in selling, emphasis must be placed on benefits that contribute to the company's goals such as:

- Aiding the company in reaching its goals and objectives by improving management's ability to obtain required information by making data available and timely. This increases management's ability to make knowledgeable decisions.
- Establishing plans which tie data planning and system development with business requirements. This provides management with the data they require within the appropriate time frame.

Selling End-Users

The objective in selling end-users is to present data planning and data/data base administration (DDBA) as important aids which can help them operate more effectively and efficiently. End-users are critical to the successful implementation of DDBA and data planning, and to managing the company's data resource. End-users must understand that:

- They are responsible for ensuring the integrity of the data they create and maintain, and responsible for assisting MIS in reducing redundant data and the redundant collection of the data.
- Data planning addresses information requirements in the context of a synergistic approach which makes data available on a predefined schedule as part of MIS's tactical plans. This allows end-users and system developers to be able to plan on the availability of data.

These capabilities enable individuals with a need to know to find out if the data needed exists in the company and if it exists in a mechanized form. It enables the end-user who needs data immediately to find from one source if the information exists, its characteristics, and how it can be obtained. End-users must be convinced that data/data base administration increases their ability to get the data they need, when they need it, and with greater accuracy.

Selling MIS

MIS is often the most difficult to sell. Data/data base administration (DDBA) is a threat because it puts structure into the unstructured process of data base design. System/programmer analysts often believe that their job is being simplified and will become less creative and challenging, and it will. That is problem! The primary objective in selling MIS is the issue of MIS's role in the company's business environment. To succeed, the primary factors are:

- DDBA becomes the focal point of a "company's" information policies. They recommend to management new policies and modification of existing policies; and are part of the information policy enforcement and documentation relative to these policies.
- MIS affects the company's profit and loss picture whenever hardware and software is purchased. Purchases must be based on satisfying the company's strategic and tactical plans so costs are kept in line with business goals.
- System development and maintenance costs can be reduced by sharing data and designing data bases for multiple systems. Systems are designed to use the data planning developed data bases rather than the data base designed to satisfy the system.
- Data planning affects system planning because DDBA would know if the data required to support new systems or changes to an existing system is available or would be available, based on current or planned systems developments. If the data are not available than the system's scope will have to be expanded to collect the data.

MIS can take the lead by establishing data/data base administration to develop more effective data bases through data planning and data modeling. Since there is no way to slow or stop system development, a 3 + year data planning effort should be established to identify and define the company's data environment. Continuing to solve end-users information requirements by building a system for each set of end-users needs, will continue the problems that exist today. This system-by-system approach is driving end-users to use microcomputers so they can bypass MIS because of MIS's inability to provide them with the data they require in the form they want, when they need it.

DATA PLANNING

Data planning begins by getting the commitment of at least one company executive to commit the people resources required to develop a data plan for a business function under their control. It requires a formal letter written to the managers telling them that the project is supported by him/her and that they are to assist. Once this commitment is made the project can begin.

To begin, a project team is formed which consists of not more than two MIS people and at least one end-user, preferably two. The MIS people require knowledge of the data planning approach and data normalization. The end-users should be knowledgeable in the business function, not necessarily data planning and data normalization techniques. The team of four begins by interviewing end-users whose organizations perform the tasks and activities related to the business function. Developing the business model (see Chapter 2) requires interviewing 10–20 end-users to determine the business function's processes and information requirements. It takes 3–5 weeks to complete the business model.

Next, the team begins building the data inventory by conducting one-half-day to one-day workshops on each information requirement. Before these sessions are planned, the company's organization chart is reviewed to determine which managers' groups require the information and are required at the workshops. All other managers' groups are invited to attend. At these workshops a "blue sky" or "green light" session is held to identify the detailed data inventory which supports the information requirement and to gather information required to build the normalized data model defined in Chapter 3. These workshops are scheduled with 2 days between them so the team can analyze the information and document it in the data dictionary.

Upon completion of the workshop, which takes approximately 2 months, actual data normalization begins. The normalization process is best done by spending 4–5 hours each day normalizing the data inventory from the workshops, with the remainder of the day spent with end-users to answer any questions which come up during the normalization process. Three to five months are required to complete the normalized data model. A typical business function data model contains approximately 350 normalized entities, 2000 data items, and 1500 relations between the entities.

The final step integrates the results of data planning with system development plans. For each system under development or modification, identify the information requirements from the data plan which it creates, updates, or retrieves. For the information requirements it updates or retrieves, identify the system(s) which create and update those information requirements. If any of the systems are planned to be developed, are they planned to be implemented prior to this system? If so, no change is made to the system development plans. If not, management should change priorities or face the problem of expanding the scope of this system to include the collection and maintenance of the data. Not facing up to this reality prior to system development will cause the system to exceed its budget and time frames.

DATA MODELING

Data modeling is a bottom-up approach which begins with one system and is expanded as other systems develop their normalized, usage, and structural data models. The resulting normalized data model represents the company's view of data rather than any particular business function or system. To get started, this approach requires only MIS personnel to be sold. Since data modeling is done as part of system development, the end-user and company management are already committed to the project and are not concerned with how the data base is designed. Using this approach the data base for the system is designed faster and is a more efficient than by using current, non–data modeling data base design approaches.

Data modeling requires a central Data Administration function since the normalized data model from one system is used as a basis for the next system. A central function facilitates the sharing of the model and the knowledge gained during the previous normalization efforts. The data analyst is responsible for collecting the systems data requirements during the system's system analysis phase. These requirements are reviewed and compared to the existing normalized data model(s) to identify new data, which are normalized into the existing normalized data model(s). New entities and relations are created as well as changes to existing normalized entities and relations. New data added to an entity and new relations between entities in the normalized data model are not a problem, but splitting an entity or changing an existing relation will cause a change to the existing physical data base(s) which can result in a change being required in programs using the entity or relation. This is where the data planning approach has a distinct advantage, it takes into consideration all end-user and potential system data requirements for the business function being analyzed. Data modeling does not.

In data modeling, usage data models are developed for each new system but not combined with the previous usage data models. The data base administration organization uses the new usages to evaluate the impact of the new system on the existing physical data bases that it may use. The physical data base designer uses this information with the revised structural data model and the current physical data base to determine what data bases should be modified, shared or duplicated. The usage model is also used to performance tune the physical data base design.

When new entities and relations or changes are made to the existing entities and relations in the normalized data model, the structural data model is redone. This provides the physical data base designer with a new logical data structures which are used to determine the changes required to the existing physical data base design. Once again, the choices are:

1. Duplicate the data bases (the current data bases and new data bases handling the revised logical data structure)
2. Share data bases by changing the original data bases to include the revised logical data structures
3. Some combination of the two choices

CONCLUSION

It takes longer to achieve the company's goals for data/data base administration by taking the data modeling approach than it does by implementing the data planning approach. The primary reason for recommending data planning is the concept of synergy. The synergistic approach defines the whole and then breaks it into implementable pieces which fit together. Data modeling uses the concept of integration which builds the pieces then attempts to make them fit. The integration approach works, but some shaving and fitting is required to make it work. This does not occur with data planning since it is a synergistic approach.

APPENDIX A. DOCUMENTATION EXAMPLE

NORMALIZED DATA MODEL

Entity Data Item Lists

ENTITY: BILL OF LADING
PK: Bill of Lading Number
    Bill of Lading Date
'D' Total Number of Cases
'D' Total Number of Items
'D' Total Full Case Weight
'D' Bill of Lading Total Weight
    Shipped Date
'D' Bill of Lading Total Amount
    Additions to Total Amount
    Deductions to Total Amount

ENTITY: BILL OF LADING—
FREIGHT
PK: Bill of Lading Number
PK: Freight Code Number
'D' Number of Full Cases
'D' Weight of Full Case
'D' Number of Loose Cases
'D' Weight of Loose Case

ENTITY: BILL OF LADING—
PRODUCT
PK: Bill of Lading Number
PK: Product Number
    Number of Cases
    Product Shipping Weight
'D' Total Weight of Cases
    Quantity Shipped
    Shipping List Price
'D' Product Shipment Status

ENTITY: CARRIER
PK: Carrier Number
    Carrier Name
    Carrier Billing Address
    Carrier Contact Phone Number
    Carrier Terms
    Type of Carrier

ENTITY: CARRIER—GEOGRAPHIC
LOCATION
PK: Carrier Number
PK: Zip Code
    Routing Mode
    Routing Rate
    Routing Weight

ENTITY: CUSTOMER
PK: Customer Number
    Customer Name
    DUNS Number
    Credit Rating
    Account Status
    Account Last Activity Date
    Bank Reference
    Tax Status
    Priority Code
    Credit Authorization Date
    Credit Authorization Amount
    Shipping Code
    Shipping Instructions
'D' Net Sales Dollars

'D' Gross Sales Dollars
'D' New Credit/Return Dollars
'D' Gross Credit/Return Dollars

ENTITY: CUSTOMER
ADDRESS
PK: Main Customer Number
PK: Customer Address Line 1
PK: Zip Code
    Customer Address Line 2
    Customer Address Line 3
    Customer Address Line 4

ENTITY: FREIGHT
PK: Freight Code
    Freight Description

ENTITY: GEOGRAPHIC
LOCATION
PK: Zip Code
    City Name
    State Name
    County Name

ENTITY: INVOICE
PK: Invoice Number
    Invoice Date
    Invoice Terms Percent
    Invoice Terms Description
    Cash Discount Amount
    Cash Discount Date

ENTITY: ORDER
PK: Order Number
    Customer Order Number
    Order Request Date
    Special Instructions
    Order Type
    Order Date
'D' Total Order Dollars
'D' Net Order Dollars
    Order Credit Approval
    Order Promised Date
    Order Received Date

Order Release Date
Order Status Date
Order Status

ENTITY: PRODUCT
PK: Product Number
    Product Description
    Product Price Amount
    Product Retail Price
    Product Status
    Product Status Effective Date
    Minimum Sell Quantity
    Product Name
    Quantity Per Case
    Case Weight

ENTITY: PRODUCT LINE
PK: Product Line Code
    Product Line Name

ENTITY: ORDER—
PRODUCT LINE
PK: Product Line Code
PK: Order Number
'D' Product Line Total Dollars

ENTITY: PRODUCT—ORDER
PK: Order Number
PK: Product Number
    Product Order Quantity
    Product Order List Price
    Back Order Code

ENTITY: PRODUCT—
WAREHOUSE
PK: Warehouse Number
PK: Product Number
    Quantity in Warehouse
'D' Number of Cases in Ware-
    house
'D' Number of Loose Items
    Reorder Quantity
    Reorder Placed Date

ENTITY: REGION
PK: Region Code
    Region Name
'D' Total Region Net Sales
    Amount
'D' Total Region Gross Sales
    Amount

ENTITY: RETURN/CREDIT
PK: Authorization Number
PK: Customer Number
    District Manager Approval
    Region Manager Approval
    Return/Credit Request Date
    Return/Credit Approval Date
'D' Total Return/Credit Amount
    Adjustable Description
    Adjustment Amount
'D' Net Return/Credit Amount
    Date Return/Credit Received
    Person Receiving Returns

ENTITY: RETURN/CREDIT—
PRODUCT
PK: Authorization Number
PK: Customer Number
PK: Product Number
    Return/Credit Quantity

ENTITY: SALES REPRESENTATIVE
PK: Sales Representative Number
    Sales Representative Name
'D' Gross Sales by Sales Rep.
'D' Net Sales by Sales Rep.

ENTITY: WAREHOUSE
PK: Warehouse Number
    Warehouse Address
    Floor Space
    Number of Bins Locations
    Working Hours
    Number of Employees

Entity, Data Item, and Relation Descriptions

Entity Name:	BILL OF LADING
Description:	Identifies the basic shipping document required when a customer's shipment is sent via a carrier
Entity Type:	Normalized
Business Functions Supported:	Order Processing, Order Entry, Distribution
Composed of:	PK: Bill of Lading Number
	PK: Bill of Lading Date
	'D' Total Number of Cases
	'D' Total Number of Items
	'D' Total Full Case Weight
	'D' Bill of Lading Total Weight
	Shipping Date
	Bill of Lading Total Amount
	Additions to Total Amount
	Deductions to Total Amount

Entity Name:	BILL OF LADING—PRODUCT
Description:	Identifies the product and product quantities shipped to a customer as indicated on the bill of lading
Entity Type:	Normalized
Business Functions Supported:	Order Processing, Order Entry, Distribution
Composed of:	PK: Bill of Lading Number
	PK: Product Number
	Number of Cases
	Product Shipping Weight
	'D' Total Weight of Cases
	Quantity Shipped
	Shipping List Price
	'D' Product Shipment Status

Data Item Name:	Bill of Lading Number
Description:	A descriptive code identifying a Bill of Lading sent to a Customer. The first 3 characters identify the year and month alpha code and the last 4 identify the sequence number.
Synonym:	Not applicable
Derivation:	Not applicable
Standard Value Set:	7 characters,
Format:	NNA-NNNN (yy, A through L, 0001 - 9999)

Data Item Name:	Bill of Lading Date
Description:	The date of issue for a bill of lading which is identified by a bill of lading number
Synonym:	Not applicable
Derivation:	Not applicable
Standard Value Set:	6 numerics, the first two are 01 to 12, the next two are 00 to 31, and the last two are 00 to 99.
Format:	mm–dd–yy (NN–NN–NN)

Data Item Name:	Total Number of Cases
Description:	A count of the number of cases to be shipped. These are the actual boxes, drums, etc. shipped, regardless of the number of boxes contained in the case.
Synonym:	Not applicable
Derivation:	Sum of the number of cases from the BILL OF LADING —PRODUCT entity for a given Bill of Lading Number.

Standard Value Set:	4 numerics
Format:	NNNN

Data Item Name:	Total Number of Items
Description:	A count of the number of items for all products for a specific Bill of Lading Number.
Synonym:	Not applicable
Derivation:	Sum of Product Order Quantity from the PRODUCT —ORDER entity for all products ordered and shipped for a given Bill of Lading Number.
Standard Value Set:	7 characters
Format:	N,NNN,NNN

Data Item Name:	Total Full Case Weight
Description:	The total weight of all full cases shipped under a bill of lading
Synonym:	Not applicable
Derivation:	Sum of the Weight of Full Case from the BILL OF LADING—FREIGHT entity.
Standard Value Set:	8 characters
Format:	NN,NNN,NNN

Data Item Name:	Bill of Lading Total Weight
Description:	The total weight of all cases (full and partial) shipped under a bill of lading. Used to assist in determining shipping costs.
Synonym:	Not applicable
Derivation:	Sum of the Weight of Loose Case from the BILL OF LADING—FREIGHT entity and the Total Full Case Weight from the BILL OF LADING entity.
Standard Value Set:	9 characters
Format:	NNN,NNN,NNN

Data Item Name:	Shipped Date
Description:	The date the items covered by the bill of lading are actually picked up by the carrier
Synonym:	Not applicable
Derivation:	Not applicable
Standard Value Set:	6 numerics, the first two are 01 to 12, the next two are 00 to 31, and the last two are 00 to 99.
Format:	mm-dd-yy (NN-NN-NN)

Data Item Name:	Bill of Lading Total Amount
Description:	The total dollar cost to the Customer for all products and related shipping, billing, and handling costs
Synonym:	Not applicable
Derivation:	Sum of Additions to Total Amount and Deductions to Total Amount from BILL OF LADING entity and Shipping List Price times Quantity Shipped from BILL OF LADING—PRODUCT entity.
Standard Value Set:	9 characters
Format:	NNN,NNN,NNN

Relation Name:	BILL OF LADING to INVOICE
Entities Connected:	(one) BILL OF LADING (one) INVOICE
Primary Key:	Bill of Lading Number Invoice Number
Relation Type:	One to one

Relation Name:	BILL OF LADING to BILL OF LADING—PRODUCT
Entities Connected:	(one) BILL OF LADING (many) BILL OF LADING—PRODUCT
Primary Key:	Bill of Lading Number
Relation Type:	One to many

Relation Name:	BILL OF LADING to BILL OF LADING—FREIGHT
Entities Connected:	(one) BILL OF LADING (many) BILL OF LADING—FREIGHT
Primary Key:	Bill of Lading Number
Relation Type:	One to many

Relation Name:	BILL OF LADING to WAREHOUSE
Entities Connected:	(many) BILL OF LADING (one) WAREHOUSE
Primary Key:	Bill of Lading Number Warehouse Number
Relation Type:	One to many

Relation Name:	BILL OF LADING to BILL OF LADING
Entities Connected:	(one) BILL OF LADING (many) BILL OF LADING
Primary Key:	Bill of Lading Number

Relation Type:	One to many
Description:	Used to group a number of shipments to different customers in the same city for shipment by one carrier from the same warehouse to that city. Local Carriers distribute the individual shipments to the customers under the original invoice's bill of lading.

Relation Name:	BILL OF LADING to CARRIER
Entities Connected:	(many) BILL OF LADING (one) CARRIER
Primary Key:	Bill of Lading Number Carrier Number
Relation Type:	One to many

Relation Name:	Ship Via
Entities Connected:	(one) CARRIER (many) ORDER
Primary Key:	Carrier Number Order Number
Relation Type:	One to many
Description:	This relation is used when the customer specifies, on the order, which carrier they want to have deliver the order.

Relation Name:	CUSTOMER to SALES REPRESENTATIVE
Entities Connected:	(many) CUSTOMER (many) SALES REPRESENTATIVE
Primary Key:	Customer Number Sales Representative Number
Relation Type:	Many to many

Linkage Diagram

USAGE DATA MODEL

Volume Estimates

Document:

- Entity occurrences
- Relation occurrences

These estimates assist in determining access statistics and phsical data base space requirements.

Access Statements Documentation

Describes data required by the lowest level access-critical functions, including the data items accessed, the entry or identifier data item(s), the action performed on the data items accessed, and the access frequency for each data access.

Entity Usage/Derivable Data Reports

Provides a cross reference between each entity required and the access-critical functions using it. In addition, a cross reference between derivable data used and the access-critical functions is produced. This report indicates what access-critical functions require the derivable data and what functions update it.

Entity	Average Volume	Minimum Volume	Maximum Volume	Yearly Growth
BILL OF LADING	22,000	8,000	40,000	7.0%
BILL OF LADING - FREIGHT	170,000	-	-	7.0%
CARRIER	500	-	-	1.0%
CARRIER - GEOGRAPHIC LOCATION	4,500	-	-	2.0%
CUSTOMER	8,500	-	-	10.0%
CUSTOMER ADDRESS	11,400	-	-	8.5%
FREIGHT	11	-	-	0.0%
GEOGRAPHIC LOCATION	900	-	-	0.0%
INVOICE	23,000	-	40,000	7.0%
ORDER	21,000	-	35,000	7.0%
ORDER - PRODUCT LINE	150,000	-	-	3.0%
PRODUCT	3,000	-	-	3.0%
PRODUCT - BILL OF LADING	185,000	-	420,000	7.5%
PRODUCT LINE	186	-	-	1.5%
PRODUCT ORDER	400,000	-	890,000	7.0%
PRODUCT - WAREHOUSE	75,000	1,000	150,000	3.5%
REGION	16	-	-	0.0%
RETURN/CREDIT	1,600	1,200	3,200	-0.5%
RETURN/CREDIT - PRODUCT	8,000	-	-	-0.5%
SALES REPRESENTATIVE	1,200	-	-	2.5%
WAREHOUSE	50	-	-	0.1%

Entity Occurrences Report

FROM ENTITY \ TO ENTITY	BILL OF LADING	BILL OF LADING - FREIGHT	CARRIER	CARRIER - GEO LOCATION	CUSTOMER
BILL OF LADING	-[1]	7[2]	1.1[3]	NR	NR
BILL OF LADING - FREIGHT	1	NR	NR	NR	NR
CARRIER	-[4]	NR	NR	9[5]	NR
CARRIER - GEOGRAPHIC LOCATION	NR	NR	1	NR	NR
CUSTOMER	NR	NR	NR	NR	NR
CUSTOMER ADDRESS (SHIP TO)	NR	NR	NR	NR	1.1[6]
CUSTOMER ADDRESS (BILL TO)	NR	NR	NR	NR	1.8[7]
FREIGHT	NR	1,500[8]	NR	NR	NR
GEOGRAPHIC LOCATION	NR	NR	NR	4	NR
INVOICE	1	NR	NR	NR	NR
ORDER	1.3*	NR	1*	NR	1
ORDER - PRODUCT LINE	NR	NR	NR	NR	NR
PRODUCT	NR	NR	NR	NR	NR
PRODUCT - BILL OF LADING	1	NR	NR	NR	NR
PRODUCT LINE	NR	NR	NR	NR	20,000[9]
PRODUCT ORDER	NR	NR	NR	NR	NR
PRODUCT - WAREHOUSE	NR	NR	NR	NR	NR
REGION	NR	NR	NR	NR	NR
RETURN/CREDIT	NR	NR	NR	NR	1*
RETURN/CREDIT - PRODUCT	1	NR	NR	NR	NR

*	Can be zero	1	Range 1 to 35
2	Maximum 11	3	Range 1 to 5
4	Range 0 to 500	5	Range 1 to 210
6	Range 1 to 21	7	Range 1 to 8
8	Maximum 22,000	9	Maximum 30,000

Part 1 of 5 Relation Occurrences Report

TO ENTITY / FROM ENTITY	CUSTOMER ADDRESS	FREIGHT	GEO. LOCATION	INVOICE	ORDER
BILL OF LADING	NR	NR	NR	1	1
BILL OF LADING - FREIGHT	NR	1	NR	NR	NR
CARRIER	NR	NR	NR	NR	540[1]
CARRIER - GEOGRAPHIC LOCATION	NR	NR	1	NR	NR
CUSTOMER	1[2]	NR	NR	NR	2.3[3]
CUSTOMER ADDRESS	NR	NR	1	NR	NR
FREIGHT	NR	NR	NR	NR	NR
GEOGRAPHIC LOCATION	58[4]	NR	NR	NR	NR
INVOICE	NR	NR	NR	NR	1
ORDER	NR	NR	NR	1.3	NR
ORDER - PRODUCT LINE	NR	NR	NR	NR	1
PRODUCT	NR	1	NR	NR	NR
PRODUCT - BILL OF LADING	NR	NR	NR	NR	NR
PRODUCT LINE	NR	NR	NR	NR	NR
PRODUCT ORDER	NR	NR	NR	NR	1
PRODUCT - WAREHOUSE	NR	NR	NR	NR	NR
REGION	NR	NR	43[5]	NR	NR
RETURN/CREDIT	NR	NR	NR	NR	NR
RETURN/CREDIT - PRODUCT	NR	NR	NR	NR	NR
SALES REPRESENTATIVE	NR	NR	1.7[6]	NR	40*
WAREHOUSE	NR	NR	20	NR	NR

*	Can be zero	1	Range 0 to 900
2	One for both SHIP TO and BILL TO	3	Maximum 12
4	Maximum 210	5	Maximum 58
6	Maximum 6		

Part 2 of 5 Relation Occurrences Report

TO ENTITY	
FROM ENTITY	WAREHOUSE
BILL OF LADING	NR
BILL OF LADING -	
FREIGHT	NR
CARRIER	NR
CARRIER -	
GEOGRAPHIC LOCATION	NR
CUSTOMER	NR
CUSTOMER ADDRESS	NR
FREIGHT	NR
GEOGRAPHIC LOCATION	1
INVOICE	NR
ORDER	NR
ORDER -	
PRODUCT LINE	NR
PRODUCT	NR
PRODUCT -	
BILL OF LADING	NR
PRODUCT LINE	NR
PRODUCT ORDER	NR
PRODUCT -	
WAREHOUSE	1
REGION	NR
RETURN/CREDIT	1
RETURN/CREDIT -	
PRODUCT	NR
SALES REPRESENTATIVE	NR
WAREHOUSE	NR

Part 5 of 5 Relation Occurrences Report

Business Function	Process Name	Activity Name
ACCOUNTING	BILLING	GENERATE INVOICES GENERATE BACK-ORDERS
SALES	CUSTOMER SERVICE	DETERMINE ORDER STATUS

Critical Business Process List

Business Function:	Sales
Process:	Customer Service
Activity:	Determine Orders Received
Activity Occurrence Rate:	Daily

RETRIEVE   Product Number   FOR Range of Values OF   Order Date
           Order Number
           Customer Number
           Order Date
           Product Order Quantity
           Product Order List Price

HAPPENS 2 TIMES-PER PROCESS/ACTIVITY OCCURRENCE

The only possible Entry Entity is ORDER.

ENTITY	DATA LIST DATA ITEMS	ACCESS DATA ITEM	ACCESS MODE
ORDER	Order Number Order Date	Order Date	non-key
PRODUCT - ORDER	Product Number Product Order Quantity Product Order List Price		relation
CUSTOMER	Customer Number		relation

Access Statement Documentation

Business Function: Sales

Process: Customer Service

Activity: Determine Order Status

Activity Occurrence Rate: Daily

RETRIEVE   Product Number   FOR Specific Values OF   Order Number
           Product Order Quantity
           Customer Number
           Customer Name
           Customer Address (Bill To)
           Order Date
           Order Request Date
           Order Status Date
           Order Status
           Shipping Mode

HAPPENS   180   TIMES-PER PROCESS/ACTIVITY OCCURRENCE

Possible entry entities: ORDER, ORDER - PRODUCT LINE and PRODUCT - ORDER

ORDER is the Entry Entity.

ENTITY	DATA LIST DATA ITEMS	ACCESS DATA ITEM	ACCESS MODE
ORDER	Order Date Order Request Date Order Status Date Order Status	Order Number	Primary key
PRODUCT - ORDER	Product Number Product Order Quantity		relation
CUSTOMER	Customer Number Customer Name		relation
CUSTOMER ADDRESS	Customer Address Line 1 Customer Address Line 2 Customer Address Line 3 Customer Address Line 4 State Name Zip Code		relation (Bill To)

Access Statement Documentation

Business Function: Sales

Process: Customer Service

Activity: Determine Shipments Made

Activity Occurrence Rate: Weekly

RETRIEVE Bill Of Lading Number   FOR Range Of Values OF Shipped Date
          Order Number
          Customer Name
          Total Order Dollars
          Order Date
          Order Promised Date
        - Order Request Date
          Shipped Date

HAPPENS 3 TIMES-PER PROCESS/ACTIVITY OCCURRENCE

The only possible Entry Entity is BILL OF LADING

ENTITY	DATA LIST DATA ITEMS	ACCESS DATA ITEM	ACCESS MODE
BILL OF LADING	Bill Of Lading Number Shipped Date	Shipped Date	non-key
ORDER	Order Number Total Order Dollars Order Date Order Promised Date Order Request Date		relation
CUSTOMER	Customer Name		relation

Access Statement Documentation

Business Function: Sales

Process: Customer Service

Activity: Determine Inventory Availability

Activity Occurrence Rate: Weekly

RETRIEVE   Quantity In Warehouse FOR Specific Values OF Product Number
           Product Number
           Warehouse Number
           Number Of Cases In Warehouse
           Reorder Quantity
           Reorder Placed Date

HAPPENS 30 TIMES-PER PROCESS/ACTIVITY OCCURRENCE

Possible entry entities: PRODUCT, PRODUCT ORDER, PRODUCT - BILL OF
                          LADING, and PRODUCT - WAREHOUSE.

PRODUCT - WAREHOUSE is the Entry Entity.

ENTITY	DATA LIST DATA ITEMS	ACCESS DATA ITEM	ACCESS MODE
PRODUCT - WAREHOUSE	Warehouse Number Product Number Quantity In Warehouse Number Of Cases In Warehouse Reorder Quantity Reorder Placed Date	Product Number	Primary key

Access Statement Documentation

Business Function:	Sales
Process:	Customer Service
Activity:	Change Order Information
Activity Occurrence Rate:	Daily

MODIFY   Order (entity)   FOR Specific Values OF Product Number
            Product - Order (entity)   Order Number

HAPPENS 20 TIMES-PER PROCESS/ACTIVITY OCCURRENCE

Possible entry entities: PRODUCT, PRODUCT - ORDER, PRODUCT - WAREHOUSE,
                              PRODUCT - BILL OF LADING and ORDER.

PRODUCT - ORDER is the Entry Entity.

ENTITY	DATA LIST DATA ITEMS	ACCESS DATA ITEM	ACCESS MODE
PRODUCT - ORDER	Order Number Product Number Product Order Quantity Product Order List Price Back Order Code	Order Number Product Number	Primary key Primary key
ORDER	Order Number Customer Order Number Order Request Date Special Instructions Order Type Order Date Total Order Dollars Net Order Dollars Order Credit Approval Order Promised Date Order Received Date Order Release Date Order Status Date Order Status		relation

Access Statement Documentation

Business Function: Sales
Process: Customer Service
Activity: Determine Order Status
Activity Occurrence Rate: Daily

RETRIEVE   Customer Number   FOR Range Of Values OF   Order Request Date
           Bill Of Lading Number   Shipped Date
           Order Number
           Order Request Date
           Total Order Dollars
           Order Date

HAPPENS   3   TIMES-PER PROCESS/ACTIVITY OCCURRENCE

ORDER and BILL OF LADING are the Entry Entities.

ENTITY	DATA LIST DATA ITEMS	ACCESS DATA ITEM	ACCESS MODE
ORDER	Order Number Total Order Dollars Order Date Order Request Date	Order Request Date	non-key
BILL OF LADING	Bill Of Lading Number	Shipped Date	non-key
CUSTOMER	Customer Number		relation

Access Statement Documentation

Business Function:	Sales
Process:	Ordering Products
Activity:	Add New Orders
Activity Occurrence Rate:	Daily

ADD   Order Data   FOR Specific Values OF   Customer Number
           (see Order Form)

HAPPENS   200   TIMES-PER PROCESS/ACTIVITY OCCURRENCE

The only possible Entry Entity is CUSTOMER.

ENTITY	DATA LIST DATA ITEMS	ACCESS DATA ITEM	ACCESS MODE
CUSTOMER	Customer Number	Customer Number	Primary key
ORDER	"All Data Items"		relation
PRODUCT - ORDER	Product Number Product Order Quantity Product Order Price List		relation

Access Statement Documentation

Business Function:	Sales
Process:	Customer Service
Activity:	Add New Customer
Activity Occurrence Rate:	Daily

ADD   Customer Data   FOR Specific Values OF   Customer Number
        (see Customer Data Form)

HAPPENS 1 TIMES-PER PROCESS/ACTIVITY OCCURRENCE

The only possible Entry Entity is CUSTOMER.

ENTITY	DATA LIST DATA ITEMS	ACCESS DATA ITEM	ACCESS MODE
CUSTOMER	Customer Number Customer Name DUNS Number Credit Rating Bank Reference Tax Status Credit Authorization Date Credit Authorization Amount Shipping Code Shipping Instructions	Customer Number	Primary key
CUSTOMER ADDRESS	"All Data Items"		Ship To relation
CUSTOMER ADDRESS	"All Data Items"		Bill To relation
GEOGRAPHIC LOCATION	Zip Code		relation
SALES REPRESENTATIVE	Sales Representative Name		relation

Access Statement Documentation

Business Function:	Manufacturing	
Process:	Inventory Control	
Activity:	Update Inventory	
Activity Occurrence Rate:	Daily	

UPDATE   Product Number   FOR Specific Values OF   Product Number
            Warehouse Number   Warehouse Number
            Quantity in Warehouse
            Number Of Cases in Warehouse
            Number Of Loose Items
            Reorder Placed Date

HAPPENS 10,000 TIMES-PER PROCESS/ACTIVITY OCCURRENCE

Possible entry entities: PRODUCT, PRODUCT ORDER, RETURN/CREDIT - PRODUCT,
                          PRODUCT - WAREHOUSE and BILL OF LADING - PRODUCT.

The Entry Entity is PRODUCT - WAREHOUSE

ENTITY	DATA LIST DATA ITEMS	ACCESS DATA ITEM	ACCESS MODE
PRODUCT - WAREHOUSE	Product Number Warehouse Number Quantity in Warehouse Number Of Cases in Warehouse Number Of Loose Items	Product Number Warehouse Number	Primary key Primary key

Access Statement Documentation

Business Function: Research

Process: New Product Development

Activity: Establishing A New Product

Activity Occurrence Rate: Yearly

```
ADD        Product Number          FOR Specific Values OF  Product Number
           Product Description
           Product Price Amount
           Product Retail Price
           Product Status
           Product Status Effective Date
           Minimum Sell Quantity
           Product Name
           Quantity Per Case
           Case Weight
           Freight Code
           Product Line Code
           Warehouse Number
```

HAPPENS 750 TIMES-PER PROCESS/ACTIVITY OCCURRENCE

Possible entry entities: PRODUCT, PRODUCT ORDER, RETURN/CREDIT - PRODUCT,
                          PRODUCT - WAREHOUSE and BILL OF LADING - PRODUCT.

PRODUCT is the Entry Entity.

ENTITY	DATA LIST DATA ITEMS	ACCESS DATA ITEM	ACCESS MODE
PRODUCT	"All Data Items"	Product Number	Primary key
PRODUCT - WAREHOUSE	Product Number Warehouse Number		relation
FREIGHT	Freight Code		relation
PRODUCT LINE	Product Line Code		relation

Access Statement Documentation

Business Function:	Market Research
Process:	Product Evaluation
Activity:	Remove Poor Selling Products
Activity Occurrence Rate:	Yearly

Delete   Product Number   FOR Specific Values OF Product Number
             Product Description
             Product Price Amount
             Product Retail Price
             Product Status
             Product Status Effective Date
             Minimum Sell Quantity
             Product Name
             Quantity Per Case
             Case Weight
             Freight Code
             Product Line Code
             Warehouse Number
             Quantity in Warehouse
             Number Of Cases in Warehouse
             Number Of Loose Items
             Reorder Quantity
             Reorder Placed Date

HAPPENS 450 TIMES-PER PROCESS/ACTIVITY OCCURRENCE

Possible entry entities: PRODUCT, PRODUCT ORDER, RETURN/CREDIT - PRODUCT,
                             PRODUCT - WAREHOUSE and BILL OF LADING - PRODUCT.

PRODUCT is the Entry Entity.

ENTITY	DATA LIST DATA ITEMS	ACCESS DATA ITEM	ACCESS MODE
PRODUCT	"All Data Items"	Product Number	Primary key
PRODUCT - WAREHOUSE	"All Data Items"		relation
FREIGHT	Freight Code		relation
PRODUCT LINE	Product Line Code		relation

Access Statement Documentation

```
Business Function:        Finance
Process:                  Billing
Activity:                 Produce Invoices
Activity Occurrence Rate: Daily
```

```
Retrieve   Order Number              FOR Specific Values OF   Order Number
           Customer Order Number
           Order Type
           Order Date
           Total Order Dollars
           Net Order Dollars
           Order Received Date
           Product Number
           Product Order Quantity
           Product Order List Price
           Back Order Code
           Product Name
           Quantity Per Case
           Case Weight
           Freight Code

HAPPENS   200   TIMES-PER PROCESS/ACTIVITY OCCURRENCE

Possible entry entities:  ORDER, and PRODUCT ORDER.
ORDER is the Entry Entity.
```

ENTITY	DATA LIST DATA ITEMS	ACCESS DATA ITEM	ACCESS MODE
ORDER	Order Number Customer Order Number Order Type Order Date Total Order Dollars Net Order Dollars Order Received Date	Order Number	Primary key
PRODUCT ORDER	Order Number Product Number Product Order Quantity Product Order List Price Back Order Code		relation
PRODUCT	Product Name Quantity Per Case Case Weight Freight Code		relation

Access Statement Documentation

```
Business Function:      Finance
Process:                Billing
Activity:               Produce Invoices
Activity Occurrence Rate: Daily
```

```
Retrieve  Order Number          FOR Specific Values OF  Order Number
          Customer Number
          Customer Name
          Tax Status
          Credit Authorization Amount
          Shipping Code
          Shipping Instructions
          Customer Address Line 1
          Customer Address Line 2
          Customer Address Line 3
          Customer Address Line 4
          City Name
          State Name
          Zip Code
          Carrier Number
          Routing Mode
          Routing Rate
          Routing Weight

HAPPENS  200  TIMES-PER PROCESS/ACTIVITY OCCURRENCE

Possible entry entities:  ORDER, and PRODUCT ORDER.

ORDER is the Entry Entity.
```

Access Statement Documentation

ENTITY	DATA LIST DATA ITEMS	ACCESS DATA ITEM	ACCESS MODE
ORDER	Order Number	Order Number	Primary key
CUSTOMER	Customer Number Customer Name Tax Status Credit Authorization Amount Shipping Code Shipping Instructions		relation
CUSTOMER ADDRESS	Customer Address Line 1 Customer Address Line 2 Customer Address Line 3 Customer Address Line 4 City Name State Name		Bill To relation
GEOGRAPHIC LOCATION	Zip Code		relation
CARRIER - GEOGRAPHIC LOCATION	Carrier Number Routing Mode Routing Rate Routing Weight		relation

Access Statement Documentation

Business Function: Finance
Process: Billing
Activity: Produce Invoices
Activity Occurrence Rate: Daily

Update   Order Status   FOR Specific Values OF   Order Number
            Order Status Date
            Invoice Number
            Invoice Date
            Invoice Terms Percent
            Invoice Terms Description
            Cash Discount Amount
            Cash Discount Date
            Bill Of Lading Data   (see Bill Of Lading Form)

HAPPENS   200   TIMES-PER PROCESS/ACTIVITY OCCURRENCE

Possible entry entities: ORDER, and PRODUCT ORDER.
ORDER is the Entry Entity.

ENTITY	DATA LIST DATA ITEMS	ACCESS DATA ITEM	ACCESS MODE
ORDER	Order Number	Order Number	Primary key
INVOICE	"Entire Entity Content"		relation
BILL OF LADING	"Entire Entity Content"		relation
BILL OF LADING - FREIGHT	"Entire Entity Content"		relation
FREIGHT	Freight Code		relation
CARRIER	Carrier Number		relation
PRODUCT - BILL OF	Number Of Cases Product Shipping Weight Total Weight Of Cases Quantity Shipped Shipping List Price Product Shipment Status		relation

Access Statement Documentation

Process/Activity Name	Process/Activity Occurrence Rate	Entry Data Item(s)	Access Occurrence Rate
Customer Service			
Change Order Information	Daily	Order Number, Product Number	20
Determine Inventory Availability	Weekly	Product Number	30
Determine Order Received	Daily	Order Date	2
Determine Order Status	Daily	Order Number	180
Determine Order Status	Daily	Order Request Date, Shipped Date	3
Determine Shipments Made	Weekly	Shipped Date	3
etc.			

Entity Name: ORDER Date: 5/4/8x Issue: 1

Entity Usage Report

Deriveble Data Item: Total Order Dollars Date: 5/4/8x

Component Data Items(s): Unit Price Issue: 1

Quantity Ordered Delivery Charge

Order Sales Tax

	Activity Occurrence Rate	Access Occurrence Rate
Retrieving Processes/Activities:		
Customer Service		
Determine Shipments Made	Weekly	3
Determine Order Status	Daily	3
Updating Processes/Activities:		
Change Order Information	Daily	20

Derivable Data Report

Deriveble Data Item:	Number Of Cases In Warehouse	Date:	5/4/8x
Component Data Items(s):	Quantity In Warehouse	Issue:	1
Quantity Per Case			

		Activity Occurrence Rate	Access Occurrence Rate
Retrieving Processes/Activities:			
Customer Service			
Determine Inventory Availability		Weekly	30
Updating Processes/Activities:			
None Identified			

Derivable Data Report

STRUCTURAL DATA MODEL

The Data Administrator is responsible for creating and documenting the structural model. The documentation produced includes:

- Logical structure diagrams
- Modified relationships report

Logical Data Structure Diagrams

This is the collection of the interim logical data structures created when building the structural data model as defined in Chapter 4. Each of the rules and the corresponding changes are documented with the changes noted. This provides an audit trail through the development of the structural model.

Modified Relations Report

Each decision to eliminate or modify a relation in the linkage diagram is documented. Decisions affecting the structural data model are those which can modify implied relations, or many-to-many relations. This document contains the decisions and supporting selection criteria affecting the logical data structures.

Relationship: BILL OF LADING TO CARRIER

Action Taken	Description of Modification
o Implied	A pseudo child is created because no common child or common parent exists. This new entity contains the primary key data items of the entities: BILL OF LADING, and CARRIER.
o Common Parent	
o Common Child	
X Pseudo Child	
o Identity	

Diagram Modification:

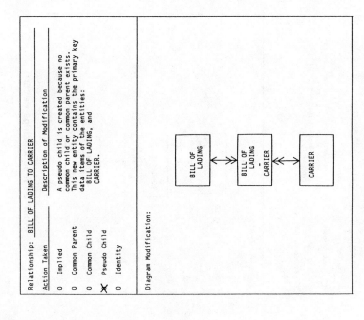

Modified Relationships Report

Relationship: ORDER TO BILL OF LADING

Action Taken	Description of Modification
X Implied	Resolved by using the relations: ORDER TO INVOICE, and INVOICE TO BILL OF LADING and passing through the entity: INVOICE.
o Common Parent	
o Common Child	
o Pseudo Child	
o Identity	

Diagram Modification:

Modified Relationships Report

Relationship: SALES REPRESENTATIVE TO GEOGRAPHIC LOCATION

Action Taken	Description of Modification
o Implied	A pseudo child is created because no
o Common Parent	common child or common parent exists. This new entity contains the primary key
o Common Child	data items of the entities: SALES REPRESENTATIVE, and
X Pseudo Child	GEOGRAPHIC LOCATION.
o Identity	

Diagram Modification:

SALES
REPRESENTATIVE

SALES
REPRESENTATIVE
-
GEOGRAPHIC
LOCATION

GEOGRAPHIC
LOCATION

Modified Relationships Report

Relationship: CUSTOMER TO PRODUCT LINE

Action Taken	Description of Modification
o Implied	A pseudo child is created because no
o Common Parent	common child or common parent exists. This new entity contains the primary key
o Common Child	data items of the entities: CUSTOMER, and
X Pseudo Child	PRODUCT LINE.
o Identity	

Diagram Modification:

CUSTOMER

CUSTOMER
-
PRODUCT
LINE

PRODUCT
LINE

Modified Relationships Report

Relationship: __INVOICE TO BILL OF LADING__

Action Taken	Description of Modification
o Implied	Remove the relation and resolve at physical
o Common Parent	data base design time. The notation:
o Common Child	I=Invoice was added to BILL OF LADING, and
o Pseudo Child	I=Bill of Lading was added to INVOICE.
X Identity	

Diagram Modification:

Modified Relationships Report

Relationship: __SALES REPRESENTATIVE TO CUSTOMER__

Action Taken	Description of Modification
o Implied	A common child entity (ORDER) satisfies
o Common Parent	the many-to-many relation. Therefore,
X Common Child	this relation is deleted from the
o Pseudo Child	logical data structures.
o Identity	

Diagram Modification:

Modified Relationships Report

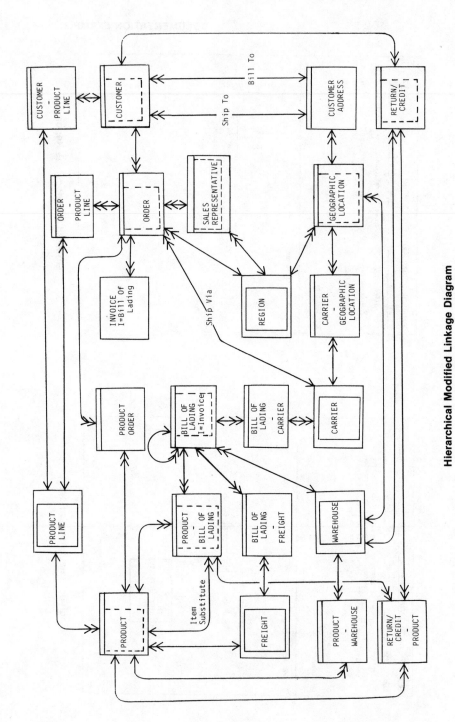

Hierarchical Modified Linkage Diagram

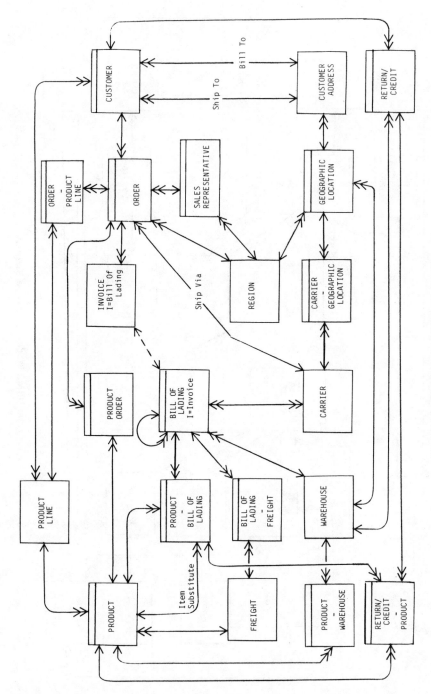

Network DBMS Modified Linkage Diagram

167

Relational DBMS Modified Linkage Diagram

Relational DBMS Entity–Data Item Lists

ENTITY: BILL OF LADING
PK: Bill of Lading Number
Bill of Lading Date
'D' Total Number of Cases
'D' Total Number of Items
'D' Total Full Case Weight
'D' Bill of Lading Total Weight
Shipped Date
'D' Bill of Lading Total Amount
Additions to Total Amount
Deductions to Total Amount
'R' Bill of Lading Number
(Composite)
'R' Carrier Number
'R' Customer Number
'R' Warehouse Number
'R' Invoice Number

ENTITY: BILL OF LADING—
FREIGHT
PK: Bill of Lading Number
PK: Freight Code
'D' Number of Full Cases
'D' Weight of Full Case
'D' Number of Loose Cases
'D' Weight of Loose Case

ENTITY: BILL OF LADING—
PRODUCT
PK: Bill of Lading Number
PK: Product Number
Number of Cases
Product Shipping Weight
'D' Total Weight of Cases
Quantity Shipped
Shipping List Price
'D' Product Shipment Status

ENTITY: CARRIER
PK: Carrier Number

Carrier Name
Carrier Billing Address
Carrier Contact Phone Number
Carrier Terms
Type of Carrier

ENTITY: CARRIER—GEOGRAPHIC
LOCATION
PK: Carrier Number
PK: Zip Code
Routing Mode
Routing Rate
Routing Weight

ENTITY: CUSTOMER
PK: Customer Number
Customer Name
DUNS Number
Credit Rating
Account Status
Account Last Activity Date
Bank Reference
Tax Status
Priority Code
Credit Authorization Date
Credit Authorization
Amount
Shipping Code
Shipping Instructions
'D' Net Sales Dollars
'D' Gross Sales Dollars
'D' New Credit/Return Dollars
'D' Gross Credit/Return Dollars

ENTITY: CUSTOMER—
PRODUCT LINE
PK: Customer Number
PK: Product Line Code

'R' Data item added to relate tables.

ENTITY: CUSTOMER ADDRESS
PK: Main Customer Number
PK: Customer Address Line 1
PK: Zip Code
    Customer Address Line 2
    Customer Address Line 3
    Customer Address Line 4
'R' Zip Code

ENTITY: FREIGHT
PK: Freight Code
    Freight Description

ENTITY: GEOGRAPHIC
LOCATION
PK: Zip Code
    City Name
    State Name
    County Name

ENTITY: INVOICE
PK: Invoice Number
    Invoice Date
    Invoice Terms Percent
    Invoice Terms Description
    Cash Discount Amount
    Cash Discount Date
'R' Order Number
'R' Bill of Lading Number

ENTITY: ORDER—PRODUCT
LINE
PK: Product Line Code
PK: Order Number
'D' Product Line Total Dollars

ENTITY: PRODUCT—ORDER
PK: Order Number
PK: Product Number
    Product Order Quantity
    Product Order List Price
    Back Order Code

ENTITY: ORDER
PK: Order Number
    Customer Order Number
    Order Request Date
    Special Instructions
    Order Type
    Order Date
'D' Total Order Dollars
'D' Net Order Dollars
    Order Credit Approval
    Order Promised Date
    Order Received Date
    Order Release Date
    Order Status Date
    Order Status
'R' Customer Number
'R' Sales Representative Number
'R' Region Code
'R' (Ship Via) Carrier Number

ENTITY: PRODUCT LINE
PK: Product Line Code
    Product Line Name

ENTITY: PRODUCT
PK: Product Number
    Product Description
    Product Price Amount
    Product Retail Price
    Product Status
    Product Status Effective
      Date
    Minimum Sell Quantity
    Product Name
    Quantity Per Case
    Case Weight
'R' Freight Code
'R' Product Line Code

ENTITY: PRODUCT—
WAREHOUSE
PK: Warehouse Number

'R' data item added to relate tables.

PK: Product Number
    Quantity in Warehouse
'D' Number of Cases in Ware-
    house
'D' Number of Loose Items
    Reorder Quantity
    Reorder Placed Date

ENTITY: REGION
PK: Region Code
    Region Name
'D' Total Region Net Sales Amount
'D' Total Region Gross Sales Amount

ENTITY: RETURN/CREDIT
PK: Authorization Number
PK: Customer Number
    District Manager Approval
    Region Manager Approval
    Return/Credit Request Date
    Return/Credit Approval Date
'D' Total Return/Credit Amount
    Adjustable Description
    Adjustment Amount
'D' Net Return/Credit Amount
    Date Return/Credit Received
    Person Receiving Returns
'R' Warehouse Number

ENTITY: RETURN/CREDIT—
PRODUCT
PK: Authorization Number
PK: Customer Number
PK: Product Number
    Return/Credit Quantity
'R' Bill of Lading Number

ENTITY: SALES
REPRESENTATIVE
PK: Sales Representative Number
    Sales Representative Name
'D' Gross Sales by Sales Rep.
'D' Net Sales by Sales Rep.
'R' Region Code

ENTITY: SALES
REPRESENTATIVE—
GEOGRAPHIC LOCATION
PK: Sales Representative Number
PK: Zip Code

ENTITY: WAREHOUSE
PK: Warehouse Number
    Warehouse Address
    Floor Space
    Number of Bins Locations
    Working Hours
    Number of Employees

'R' data item added to relate tables.

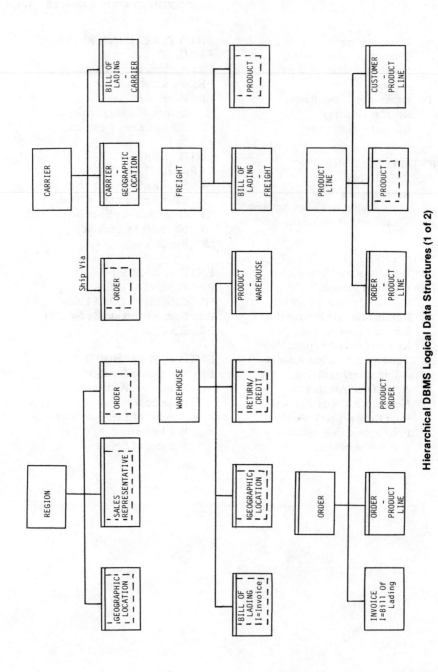

Hierarchical DBMS Logical Data Structures (1 of 2)

172

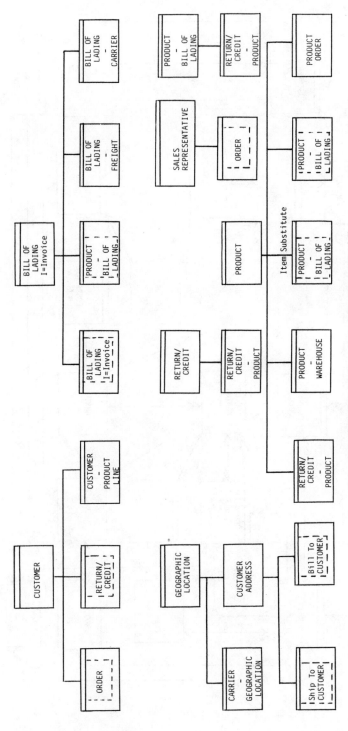

Hierarchical DBMS Logical Data Structures (2 of 2)

173

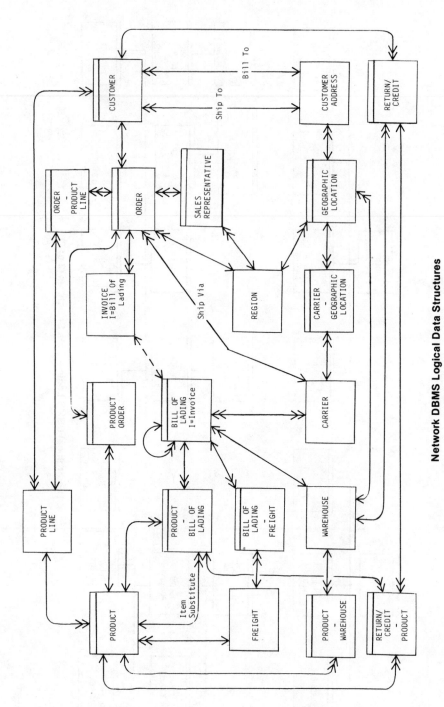

Network DBMS Logical Data Structures

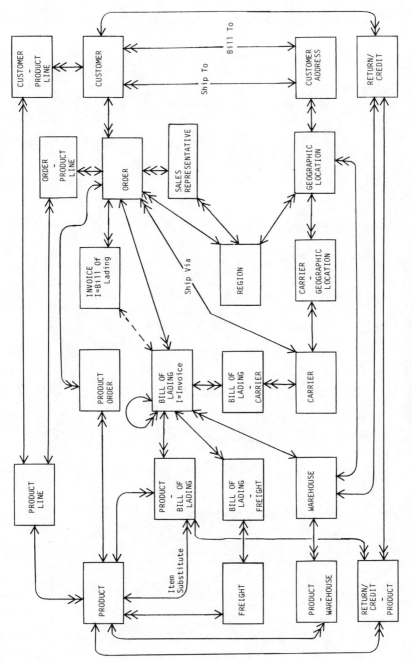

Relational DBMS Logical Data Structures

APPENDIX B: REPORT FORMATS

Entity Name:

   Description:

   Entity Type:

   Business Functions
     Supported:

   Composed Of: PK:
           PK:

- -

Entity Name:

   Description:

   Entity Type:

   Business Functions
     Supported:

   Composed Of: PK:
           PK:

- -

Entity Description

```
Data Item Name:

   Description:



   Synonym:

   Derivation:

   Standard-Value-Set:

   Format:

   Composed Of:



- - - - - - - - - - - - - - - - - - - - - - - - - - - - - - - - - -

Data Item Name:

   Description:



   Synonym:

   Derivation:

   Standard-Value-Set:

   Format:

   Composed Of:



- - - - - - - - - - - - - - - - - - - - - - - - - - - - - - - - - -
```

Data Item Description

Relation Name:

   Entities Connected:

   Primary Key:

   Relation Type:

   Description:

- -

Relation Name:

   Entities Connected:

   Primary Key:

   Relation Type:

   Description:

- -

Relation Name:

   Entities Connected:

   Primary Key:

   Relation Type:

   Description:

- -

Relation Description

```
 TO ENTITY

FROM ENTITY




















Footnotes



```

Relation Occurrences Report

Business Function	Process Name	Activity Name

Critical Business Process List

Business Function:

Process:

Activity:

Activity Occurrence Rate:

RETRIEVE ⎤
ADD   ⎟
MODIFY   ⎬   FOR ⎡ Range of Values ⎤ OF
REMOVE   ⎦   ⎨ Specific Values ⎬
                                         ⎣ All Values   ⎦

HAPPENS ___ TIMES-PER PROCESS/ACTIVITY OCCURRENCE

The possible Entry Entity(s) is(are):

ENTITY	DATA LIST DATA ITEMS	ACCESS DATA ITEM	ACCESS MODE

Access Statement Documentation

Entity Name: _____		Date: _____ Issue: _____	
Process/Activity Name	Process/Activity Occurrence Rate	Entry Data Item(s)	Access Occurrence Rate

Entity Usage Report

Derivable Data Item: _____		Date: _____	
Component Data Items(s): _____		Issue: _____	
_____ _____			
_____ _____		Activity Occurrence Rate	Access Occurrence Rate
_____ _____			
Retrieving Processes/Activities:			
Updating Processes/Activities:			

Derivable Data Report

Relationship: _____

Action Taken	Description of Modification
O Implied	
O Common Parent	
O Common Child	
O Pseudo Child	
O Identity	

Diagram Modification:

Modified Relation Report

APPENDIX C: JOB DESCRIPTIONS

POSITION DESCRIPTION

Position Title: Manager Data/Data Base Administration

Reports To: Director, Management Information Services

Description: Responsible for managing the company's data resource, which includes establishing company-wide policies and procedures for data analysis, data design, and data base related activities. Provides guidance to end-users and systems development managers on topics relating to data and data base. Enforces the use of common data structures where technically feasible and ensures maximum availability of data to authorized end-users. Responsible for data security and integrity controls and the establishment and maintenance of data/data base support tools. Manages personnel performing data planning, data modeling, data dictionary, and data base design activities.

Activities:

1. Reviews business plans and long-range system plans to determine current and evolving information needs.
2. Establishes policies and procedures defining the responsibilities of end-users, data administrators, data base administrators, systems analysts, and programmers in building, maintaining, and using data bases.
3. Recommends to management better use of data for planning, organizing, and controlling the business.
4. Responsible for establishing data analysis and data design methods and procedures used to design physical data bases.

5. Responsible for identifying and documenting data security requirements including who has the right access the data.
6. Coordinates the control over accessing and updating data.
7. Responsible for defining and implementing data base backup and recovery procedures.
8. Responsible for developing or acquiring software to facilitate design, development, testing, and maintenance of data bases.
9. Performs other related duties as assigned.

Scope of Position:

1. Manages a highly skilled staff of data analysts and data base analysts who provides technical assistance to system development personnel on the use and implementation of data bases.
2. Approval authority regarding the development and implementation of data/data base administration policies and procedures.
3. Resolves and delivers timely, accurate, and efficient data base support needed by the end-users and system developers.
4. Possesses superior written and oral communications skills with the ability to address executives, managers, and technicians.
5. Has 8 to 10 years experience in data/data base administration.

POSITION DESCRIPTION

Position Title: Manager, Data Administration

Reports To: Manager, Data/Data Base Administration

Description: Plans, organizes, and controls the development of data planning, development of the company's and systems' data models, and establishes and maintains the company's data inventory in a data dictionary. Establishes the company's data dictionary standards and procedures. Provides detailed support activities required to implement new or modified data base systems. Documents changes to the data base environment. Has custodial responsibility for the data base definitions. Ensures compliance with standards and maintains the data dictionary facilities to support system development and maintenance.

Activities:

1. Participates in management planning sessions to formulate data plans consistent with the company's short- and long-range plans.
2. Develops data administration standards, methods, and procedures.
3. Prepares action plans for establishing and maintaining an inventory of data in the company, including establishing methods and procedures for using the data dictionary to document the company's data inventory and generation of data file and data bases definitions.
4. Establishes and enforces the company's data naming standards.
5. Manages data analysts who perform data planning and data modeling.
6. Supervises data dictionary clerks who enters and maintains data descriptions contained in the data dictionary.
7. Coordinates the generation of data base and data area definitions from the data dictionary.
8. Provides training to data dictionary personnel and programming staff on the function and use of the data dictionary facilities.
9. Performs other duties as assigned.

Scope of Position:

1. Assigns and reviews work for data analysts.
2. Assigns and reviews work performed by data dictionary clerks and responsible for prioritizing work assignments.
3. Recommends hiring and dismissals, conducts performance appraisals, and performs related supervisory duties.
4. Maintains close working relationship with data base analysts, system development personnel, and end-users.
5. Maintains expertise by attending job related seminars and classes and participates in industry-wide data processing organizations.
6. Possesses superior written and oral communication skills with the ability to address both management and technical personnel.
7. Has 5 to 8 years experience in system development and Data Administration.

POSITION DESCRIPTION

Position Title: Manager, Data Base Administration

Reports To: Manager, Data/Data Base Administration

Description: Responsible for planning, organizing, controlling, and securing the company's data bases. This includes designing, implementing, monitoring, performance tuning, and securing the company's data base environment. Responsible for the selection, support, and maintenance of data base support tools, methodologies, and procedures. Ensures compliance with standards and maintains the data base entironment to support system development and maintenance.

Activities:

1. Review data analysis and data design status through periodic planned design reviews and conferences with system development managers. Recommends corrective action when necessary.
2. Establishes data base design and implementation methods and procedures consistent with data analysis methods and procedures.
3. Establishes and enforces standards for use, control, updating, and maintenance of data bases.
4. Provides support to systems utilizing data base management system software including establishing data base access and update.
5. Supervises and directs data base analysts engaged in activities such as physical data base design and the development of data base related information system standards and procedures.
6. Provides training on data base standards, methods, and procedures.
7. Maintains documentation relating to data base software and system environment changes, and maintains data base system problem tracking documentation and reporting.
8. Performs other duties as assigned.

Scope of Position:

1. Supervises data base analysts who build, implement, and maintain data bases.

2. Analyzes the impact of proposed systems on the company's data base environment.
3. Designs, implements, and maintains subject/common data bases for use by new systems based on the company's data model.
4. Evaluates and establishes distributed data bases required to satisfy end-user requirements.
5. Designs, implements, and maintains the mechanisms for effective data base back-up and recovery.
6. Designs, implements, and maintains the interface between strategic, tactical, and operational data bases.
7. Participates in the evaluation and selection of purchased systems by evaluating it data structures versus the company's data model.
8. Determines software enhancements or modifications required to support a system's data base requirements.
9. Interacts with data center personnel in determining software enhancements or modifications required to support the expanding data requirements, and implement required modifications to the data base environment.

Scope of Position:

1. Decision-making responsibility for designing and implementing efficient data bases.
2. Maintains close working relationship with data analysts, system development personnel, data center personnel, and end-users.
3. Maintains professional knowledge of the state-of-the-art in data base by attending courses and seminars, and by individual study.
4. Has 3 + years experience in physical data base design, data dictionary use and system development.

POSITION DESCRIPTION

Position Title: Data Base Technician

Reports To: Manager, Data Base Administrator

Description: Responsible for coordinating the integration of the company's physical data bases when technically feasible. Assists the data base analysts in the technical aspects of data base design and implementation. Provides technical data base management and telecommunications support by providing programming consultation, debugging assistance, and recommending technical design approaches to ensure the data bases are consistent with the company's data model and operating environment performance requirements. Provides the data base analysts and computer operations with technical expertise in the areas of DBMS system performance monitoring, analysis and tuning.

Activities:

1. Establishes state-of-the-art data design methods and procedures for migrating existing systems to a data base environment and maintaining the data base environment.
2. Analyzes the impact of proposed data bases on the company's data processing center.
3. Develops, implements, and monitors data security, integrity, and availability methods and procedures.
4. Establishes the guidelines and constraints for interfacing the company's and organization's strategic, tactical, and operational data bases.
5. Participates in the evaluation and selection of purchased systems by evaluating it data structures versus the company's data model.
6. Determines software and DBMS related enhancements or modifications required to support the company's data base environment.
7. Interacts with data center personnel in implementing DBMS and related software enhancements or modifications required to expand the capabilities of the data base environment.

Scope of Position:

1. Assist in the decision making responsibility for DBMS technical areas for designing and implementing efficient data bases.

2. Maintain close working relationship with data analysts, system development personnel, and data center personnel.
3. Maintains professional knowledge of the state-of-the-art in data base and related technical areas by attending courses and seminars, and by individual study.
4. Has 5+ years experience in physical data base design, data dictionary use and system development.

POSITION DESCRIPTION

Position Title: Data Dictionary Analyst

Reports To: Manager, Data Administration

Description: Assists data analyst, data base analyst, system development personnel, and end-users in obtaining, updating and maintaining information contained in the data dictionary. Responsible for maintaining the security of the data dictionary.

Activities:

1. Assists data analysts and data base analysts in maintaining and structuring data, data bases, files, programs and systems on the data dictionary.
2. Develops, implements, and maintains data dictionary usage and security standards, guidelines, and procedures.
3. Develops, implements, and maintains data dictionary documentation standards and guidelines.
4. Designs, implements, and maintains the mechanisms for effective data dictionary backup and recovery.
5. Coordinates and monitors the use of the data dictionary and takes appropriate action when misuse occurs or security violations are attempted.
6. Provides training to personnel requiring the ability to access, update or maintain the data dictionary content.

Scope of Position:

1. Responsible for high degree of accuracy in data dictionary use and security.
2. Maintains close working relationship with data analysts, system development personnel, data center personnel, and end-users.
3. Trained in all aspects of the data dictionary.

APPENDIX D: DATA/DATA BASE ADMINISTRATION POLICY

PURPOSE

Establish the responsibilities for effectively managing the company's data resource and ensure the most efficient use of this essential resource by the company.

SCOPE

Provisions within this policy affect all domestic and foreign organizations of the company and its subsidiaries. For the purpose of this policy, the term "Director, Management Information Services" encompasses all management information services (MIS) organizations within the company.

OBJECTIVES

1. *To service the company* by making data contained in the source documents of the company available to the managers of business.
2. *To ensure consistency of data* by establishing common terminology and standard definitions for data contained in the data resource.
3. *To ensure cost-effective use of data* by eliminating unnecessary collection and storage of data, utilizing common data bases and streamlining access to data.
4. *To ensure security of data* by establishing and enforcing data security guidelines while making data available to those authorized to have access.

DEFINITIONS

1. *Source Documents.* Any relevant record of a business event or transaction received by the company or generated for use outside the company.
2. *Data/Data Base Administration.* Establishes policy and procedures which direct the manner in which the company establishes; defines secures, and controls the use of data, files, and data bases to provide timely and accurate information for conducting business.
3. *Data Planning.* Identifies the company's information requirements, including source, definition, structure, format, and usage of data.
4. *Data Analysis.* Determines the structure of the company's data resource based on user requirements which:

   - Satisfy organizational information requirements
   - Satisfy organizational processing requirements
   - Provide a simple, comprehensive representation of data
   - Accommodate adaptation to future requirements

5. *Data Design.* Determines the computer data base structure that meets performance and security requirements for the company's information systems. The objective of data design is to balance data access flexibility with data availability.

RESPONSIBILITIES

1. *Company Management:* Ensures the integrity of the company data resource by supporting data planning, data analysis, and data design.
2. *Director of MIS:* Provides company-wide direction to data planning, data analysis, and data design by maintaining technological currency and by establishing standards and guidelines. Plans and operates company's data base operating environment.
3. *MIS Managers/Directors:* Establishes and executes cost-effective data planning, data analysis, and data design to provide timely, accurate, and accessible data to the managers of the business.

APPENDIX E: DATA/DATA BASE ADMINISTRATION CHARTER

Data/data base administration is the establishment and enforcement of policy and procedures for managing company's data resource. It is responsible for implementing an economical and technically feasible approach to manage the data resource.

GOALS

Data Planning

Develop and annually update a long-range data plan (5 years) for management of the data resource.

Company Data Dictionary

Establish a data dictionay which documents data definitions for current and future computer systems in company. The dictionary is the source for data descriptions for new systems or major rewrites of existing systems.

Data Availability

Identify and define methods for users to access data and information about data. Identify and recommend interfaces and procedures for increasing data accessibility using the information center and personal computers.

System Development Life Cycle

Integrate data administration procedures into the company's system development life cycle.

Establish Data Administration Procedures

Establish procedures for work functions in the areas of data administration. They include:

- Definition of responsibilities
- Logical data base design
- Data dictionary development and use
- Security/integrity controls
- Data definition requirements

DATA ADMINISTRATION RESPONSIBILITIES

Data Planning:

Develop and maintain a long-range data plan for the company which identifies business functions, processes, information requirements, and the company's data models.

Data Dictionary:

1. Defines and issues company data naming standards. Coordinates with technical support group naming conventions for data bases and files, as generated from the data dictionary.
2. Reviews and inures compliance with company's data dictionary standards.
3. Develops and maintains standards for interfacing the dictionary with DBMS and programming languages.
4. Documents and maintains an inventory of all data in the company which includes the source for each data item and its attributes.

Data Analysis

1. Defines, documents and uses tools and techniques required to develop the company's and system's data models.
2. Integrates data planning and data modeling methods and procedures with the company's system development process.
3. Develops and documents techniques for providing data base ad-

ministration with information needed to select the appropriate DBMS for a system.

4. Identifies and document company's security and integrity requirements for data.
5. Defines and documents a system's logical data structures (normalized data model).
6. Defines and documents a system's data usage requirements during the system analysis and system design phases (usage data base).
7. Creates the potential DBMS/file logical structures (structural data model).

Data Security

1. Establishes data access authority based on the company's data security guidelines.
2. Establishes access to data via the data base management system and data dictionary software tools.

Systems Development

1. Reviews systems and identifies potential for shared common subject data bases and opportunities for minimizing redundant data collection efforts.
2. Reviews systems and assists in identifying and defining data, data definitions, and sources of data, and in developing system data models.
3. Reviews systems to identify possibilities for common data bases.
4. Assists the system analyst in identifying and defining the systems data requirements and sources for the data using the company's data inventory.

DATA BASE ADMINISTRATION RESPONSIBILITIES

Data Dictionary

1. Authorizes and documents deviations from data administration's logical data structures.

2. Enforces system compliance to company data dictionary standards.
3. Responsible for ensuring that system internal files are documented in the data dictionary, and file and data base definitions are generated from the data dictionary.

Data Design

1. Designs, models, and implements the company's physical data bases based on the data models.
2. Creates the system's physical data base structures using data administration's data models.
3. Ensures that data bases satisfy the system's needs within the constraints of the company's data plans utilizing common and shared data bases where feasible.
4. Coordinates testing of the system's physical data bases.
5. Establishes, monitors, and performance tunes data base access and structure.
6. Determines, monitors, and performance tunes data base physical storage and CPU requirements.

Data Security

1. Uses available software and hardware tools to monitor, enforce, and secure the company's data resource.
2. Ensures that system and user access to data is in compliance with company data security guidelines.

Systems Development

1. Ensures compliance with the company's data security controls for data bases.
2. Establishes data base subschemas to support system development requirements.
3. Enforces the company's data and data base standards.
4. Establishes, monitors, and enforces the system's data security and access authority.

Software Maintenance

1. Maintains and installs data base management related software.
2. Reviews and evaluates software available to support the company's data base environment.
3. Is the interface with the vendors of data base management system and related software.

SELECTED BIBLIOGRAPHY

Atre, S. *Data Base: Structured Techniques for Design Performance and Management.* New York: John Wiley & Sons, Inc., 1980.

Auerbach Publishers Inc., Ed. *Practical Data Base Management.* Reston, Virginia: Reston Publishing Company, Inc., 1980.

Codd, E. F. "A Data Base Sublanguage Founded on the Relational Calculus." *IBM Research,* San Jose, Calif., July 26, 1971.

———. "Further Normalization of the Data Base Relational Model." *IBM Research,* San Jose, Calif., August 31, 1971.

———. "Normalized Data Base Structure: A Brief Tutorial." *IBM Research, San* Jose, Calif., November 3, 1971.

———. "Relational Completeness of Data Base Sublanguages." *IBM Research,* San Jose, Calif., March 6, 1972.

———. "Recent Investigations In Relational Data Base Systems." *IBM Research,* San Jose, Calif., April 23, 1974.

Date, C. J. *An Introduction to Database Systems,* Third Edition. Reading, Mass.: Addison-Wesley, 1981.

Gillenson, Mark L. *1981 SRI Data Administration Survey Report.* New York: IBM Systems Research Institute, June 22, 1981.

Inmon, W. H., and Friedman, L. J. *Design Review Methodology for a Data Base Environment.* Englewood Cliffs, N.J.: Prentice-Hall, 1982.

Martin, James. *Application Development Without Programmers.* Englewood Cliffs, N.J.: Prentice-Hall, 1982.

Martin, James. *Computer Data Base Organization,* First Edition. Englewood Cliffs, N.J.: Prentice-Hall, 1975.

———. *An End User's Guide to Data Base.* Englewood Cliffs, N.J.: Prentice-Hall, 1980.

———. *Principles of Data-Base Management.* Englewood Cliffs, N.J.: Prentice-Hall, 1976.

Tsichritzis, Dionysios, and Lochovsky, Frederick. *Data Models.* Englewood Cliffs, N.J.: Prentice-Hall, 1981.

Turk, Thomas A. *Data Normalization Techniques.* Data Base Management Series 23-01-09. New York: Auerbach Publishers, January, 1984.

Ullman, Jeffrey D. *Principles of Database Systems,* Second Edition. Rockville, Maryland: Computer Science Press, 1982.

GLOSSARY

Access Statement. Defines the Business Processes requirements for
data. It identifies the activity in the following format:

Business Function: function name
Process: process name
Activity: activity name
Activity Occurrence Rate: time frame

ADD
REMOVE data   Specific Values
MODIFY list FOR Range of Values OF access data items(s)
RETRIEVE   All Values

HAPPENS   number   TIMES PER ACTIVITY/PROCESS
OCCURRENCE.

Business Function. A high-level activity which is descriptive of the
basic processes and activities performed in a company. Usually it is the
responsibility of a single organization, however, it can be shared between organizations. Some examples are: finance, marketing, and
purchasing.

Business Process. A set of related activities performed in a company which supports a business function. This set of activities reflects
what has to be done not how they are done.

Custodial Rights. The responsibility for ensuring the integrity of
data including the responsibility for collecting, editing, and maintaining the data and providing access to the data by others and systems.

Child Entity.   The entity at the "many" end of a one-to-many relation is called the child.

Critical Business Process.   A business process which has one or more of the following characteristics:

- A high data access rate. This occurs when a process has many data items accesses or has many accesses against the data.
- A high function occurrence rate. This indicates the number of times the function is initiated per interval of time.
- Important to the user. These processes have higher priority relative to other processes.

Data Administration (DA).   The function responsible for identifying and defining the company's inventory of data, establishing the company's data plan, developing and documenting the company's and system's normalized, usage, and structural data models. The non–data base management system (non-DBMS) technical activities required to manage the company's data resource are done by data administration.

Data Base Administration (DBA).   The function which is responsible for the decisions and activities on the technical design and implementation of data bases on the normalized usage, and structural data models.

Data Dependency.   Indicates that an occurrence of one entity must exist before an occurrence of the other entity can exist. For every relation existing between two entities, a data dependency exists between them and the direction of the dependency is identified.

Data/Data Base Administration (DDBA).   The function responsible for centralizing the management of the company's data resource.

Direct Path.   A one-to-many or one-to-one relation which connects two entities.

Entity Usage.   Specifies for each entity the processes which access it, the access mode and activity occurrence rate.

Identity Relation. A relation between two entities which contains a simple (one-to-one) relation.

Implied Relation. A path between two entities can be implied by following an indirect path connecting the same two entities.

Indirect Path. An indirect path is a path which connects two entities by using two or more one-to-many or one-to-one relations. The flow of the indirect path is in the one-to-many direction.

Many-to-Many Relation. A relation between two entities in which a given occurrence of each entity will be related to zero, one, or more than one occurrence of the entity to which it is related.

Normalization. The process of breaking down complex end-user views of data into simple data structures that can be represent in two-dimensional arrays or tables.

Normalized Data Model. A data structure which represents data in the end-user environment. It is constructed using E. F. Codd's relational data base theory (see bibliography for references).

One-Way Dependency. The requirement for one entity connected by a relation to exist before an occurrence of the other entity can exist with the reverse not being true.

Parent Entity. The entity at the "one" end of a one-to-many relation is called the parent. In Fig. 5-1 entity A is the parent of B.

Path. A set of two or more entities which are connected by relations.

Potentially Redundant Entity. An entity which has more than one complex (many) relation entering it.

Pseudo-Root. A redundant entity which has one or more simple relations (the "one" end of a relation) entering it.

Root. An entity which has only simple relations enter it or no relations enter it.

Structural Data Model. Created from the normalized data model by manipulating the normalized data model's linkage diagram to produce logical data structures. Seven steps translate the normalized data into logical data structures that can be implemented by a nonrelational data base management system (DBMS).

Synergistic Approach. A synergistic approach is one which defines the whole environment and then breaks it into its components for implementation.

Two-Way Dependency. Each entity connected by a relation requires an occurrence of the other to exist.

Usage Data Model. Information on the use of data as perceived by the end-users, including how data is used, how often it is used, and entity and relation volume statistics. It is a collection of high-level business usage information used to design data bases.

Volume Estimates. The number of occurrences for each entity and relation in the normalized data model.

INDEX

Access Authorization, 115
Access Data Item, 56. *See also* Access
   Statement
Access Mode, 60. *See also* Access Statement
Access Requirement. *See* Access Statement
Access Statement, 54, 56, 139, 207. *See also*
   Documentation; Forms

Benefits, 11, 125
   Cost Reduction, 11
   Data Security, 12
   Data Sharing, 12
   Decision Making, 11
BSP. *See* Business System Planning
Business Function, 15, 207. *See also* Source
   Business Function
Business Function/System Matrix. *See* Doc-
   umentation
Business Process, 15, 207
Business System Planning, 15

Candidate Key, 32
CBP. See Critical Business Process
Charter. *See* Data/Data Base Administra-
   tion Charter
Child Entity. *See* Entity
Common Child. *See* Logical Data Structure
Common Logical Data Structure, 23. *See
   also* Logical Data Structure
Common Parent. *See* Logical Data Struc-
   ture
CONDOR, 107. *See also* Physical Data
   Base Design.
Cost Reduction. *See* Benefits
Critical Business Process, 50, 54, 208. *See
   also* Documentation; Forms
Custodial Rights, 22, 207

DA. *See* Data Administration
D/DBA. *See* Data/Data Base Administra-
   tion
Data Administration, 8, 109, 110, 200, 208
Data Analysis, 200
Data Analyst, 121. *See also* Job Descrip-
   tions
Data Availability. *See* Benefits
Data Base Access and Manipulation, 117
Data Base Administration, 8, 109, 208
Data Base Analyst, 121. *See also* Job De-
   scriptions.
Data Base Standards, 118
Data Dependency, 19, 208. *See also* Docu-
   mentation
Data Design, 202. *See also* Data Modeling;
   Logical Data Structure
Data Dictionary, 111, 116, 200, 201
Data Dictionary Analyst, 121. *See also* Job
   Description
Data Integrity. *See* Benefits
Data Inventory, 10, 16, 26. *See also* Docu-
   mentation
Data Item. *See* Documentation; Forms
Data Modeling
   First Normal Form, 32
   Logical Data Structure, 85, 92. *See also*
      Logical Data Structures.
   Modified Linkage Diagram, 68
   Normalization, 5, 18, 25, 31, 209
   Normalized Data Model, 5, 11, 16, 25,
      209
   Second Normal Form, 32, 38
   Structural Data Model, 7, 64, 67, 88, 210
   Third Normal Form, 32, 40
   Usage Data Model, 6, 50, 210
Data Planning, 2, 4, 12, 14, 111, 127, 200